THE
ECONOMICS
BIBLE

A FIREFLY BOOK

Published by Firefly Books Ltd. 2017

First printing

Publisher Cataloging-in-Publication Data (U.S.)

Library of Congress Cataloging-in-Publication Data is available

Library and Archives Canada Cataloguing in Publication

Pettinger, Tejvan, author
    The economics bible : the definitive guide to the science of
wealth, money and world finance / Tejvan Pettinger.
Includes index.
ISBN 978-1-77085-939-5 (softcover)
    1. Economics. I. Title.
HB171.5.P458 2017   330   C2017-902161-3

Published in the United States by
Firefly Books (U.S.) Inc.
P.O. Box 1338, Ellicott Station
Buffalo, New York 14205

Published in Canada by
Firefly Books Ltd.
50 Staples Avenue, Unit 1
Richmond Hill, Ontario L4B 0A7

Printed in China

First published by Cassell, a
division of Octopus Publishing
Group Ltd, Carmelite House,
50 Victoria Embankment,
London EC4Y 0DZ

Tejvan Pettinger asserts the
moral right to be identified as
the author of this work.
Edited and designed by
Whitefox; **Editorial Director**
Trevor Davies; **Production
Controller** Meskerem Berhane

THE ECONOMICS BIBLE

THE DEFINITIVE GUIDE TO THE SCIENCE OF WEALTH, MONEY AND WORLD FINANCE

TEJVAN PETTINGER

FIREFLY BOOKS

CONTENTS

INTRODUCTION

THE ORIGINS OF ECONOMICS

Economics is concerned with the management of scarce resources — how to make the best use of the limited raw materials that we have. The word "economics" originates from the Greek word *oikonomia*, which means "to manage your household."

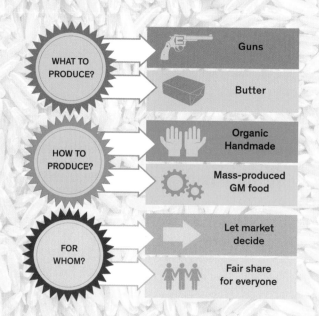

WHAT TO PRODUCE?	Guns
	Butter
HOW TO PRODUCE?	Organic Handmade
	Mass-produced GM food
FOR WHOM?	Let market decide
	Fair share for everyone

The term was used by the Greek philosopher Xenophon (431–360 BCE), who wrote about how landlords could more effectively manage their estates. Among other things, he mentioned division of labor and specialization of workers (workers given specific tasks that they concentrated on). The early Greek and Roman states also developed the concept of private property — an essential ingredient of capitalism.

There was no discipline of economics as we understand it until many centuries later, and it was often left to philosophers to consider "economic issues." For example, the Greek philosopher Plato's *Republic* was a manifesto for a just society, in which he envisaged "philosopher kings" seeking to maximize the welfare of a country. Plato (d. 348/347 BCE) didn't seem to believe in leaving it to the free market.

The earliest coins appeared around the seventh century BCE, which helped societies progress from a barter economy (for example, swapping seven hens for a sword) to more sophisticated economic systems in which individuals could specialize in certain jobs and be paid in a common currency.

Aristotle (384–322 BCE), another Greek philosopher and polymath, wrote about money as a medium of exchange and a way of providing relative value. Aristotle also mentioned a harmonious mean — a fair price agreed by buyer and seller, which is an early formulation of the law of supply and demand (see Supply and Demand, page 28).

◀ *A statue of Greek philosopher Plato.*

MERCANTILISM

In broad terms, mercantilism promoted the idea that nation states should seek to accumulate raw materials and precious metals (especially silver and gold). It also advocated government intervention in key areas of the economy, which included:

- Tariffs on imports to protect domestic industries and prevent money leaving the economy.

- The setting of rules and regulations and the subsidizing of key export industries.

▶ A stamp featuring a portrait of Sir Francis Drake.

The aim of the economy was considered to be amassing more gold. Imports were therefore discouraged, because the economy lost gold in exchange for foreign luxuries, like French silk.

Under finance minister Jean-Baptiste Colbert (1619–83), France pursued a mercantilist policy that was driven by a rivalry with the Netherlands, which, at the time, was the more successful trading nation.

STATE PIRACY

During the 16th century, monarchs often allowed and even encouraged a state-sponsored form of piracy, with men such as Sir Francis Drake attacking Spanish ships to plunder their gold (which had itself been plundered from the Aztecs). This was mercantilism in action!

Export goods

Recieve gold

France

Great Britain

◀ A country such as Great Britain hoped to become richer by exporting goods to France and receiving gold in payment.

Thomas Mun (1571-1641) was an English merchant whose *England's Treasure by Forraign Trade* (1621) was an influential manifesto for mercantilism. In simple terms, he encouraged more exports and fewer imports, arguing, among other things, that

- Imported goods that can be produced domestically should be banned,
- Luxurious imported goods should be reduced by making Englishmen have a taste for English goods.

A ZERO-SUM GAME

Mercantilism saw the economy as a zero-sum game — in other words, one person's loss is another person's gain; one person's gain is another person's loss. It is a zero-sum game because resources are finite, and the implication is that if you want to be richer, you should try to take wealth from other countries or people.

This economic thinking had profound implications for the political outlook of European nations. Mercantilism is often associated with colonialism, with European countries such as France and Great Britain increasing their wealth by monopolizing the natural resources of their colonies.

THE RETURN OF MERCANTILISM

Although it is widely considered an outdated economic theory, aspects of mercantilism have regained popularity in recent years. This has taken the form of criticism of free trade (embodied by the North American Free Trade Agreement, or NAFTA, and the trade agreements of the European Union) and the idea that the state can play a significant role in promoting business and economic development.

U.S.
33
units

GB
33
units

France
31 units

◀ *To increase their share of wealth, a country has to take from other countries. In this case, Great Britain takes 2 units of gold from France to achieve 35 units and France falls to 31.*

When GB achieves 35 units, France is forced to reduce their share to 31 units

CLASSICAL ECONOMICS

Classical economics centers on the belief that free markets and free trade increase efficiency and prosperity. In the 18th and 19th centuries, economies were transformed by the Industrial Revolution, which brought rapid economic growth and social change. This economic change also saw the emergence of a coherent theory of classical "free-market" economics, articulated by economists such as the Britons Adam Smith (1723–90) and David Ricardo (1772–1823), and the Frenchman Jean-Baptiste Say (1767–1832).

This was in contrast to previous mercantilist theories, because it implied that countries could increase their wealth without the accumulation of gold (plundered from other countries). Classical economists believed that free trade benefits everyone, and therefore that we don't trade in a zero-sum world — in other words, if one country gains, it doesn't mean that another country has to lose out.

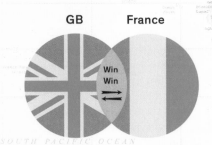

GB   France

Win
Win

◀ Trade is not a zero-sum game — there is room for both countries to benefit.

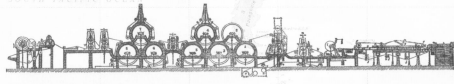

This economic theory also has implications for politics — rather than seeing other countries as rivals, it is possible to have mutually beneficial relationships that enrich all parties.

Classical economists also argued against excessive government regulation. They believed that flexible prices would enable markets to reach equilibrium (where supply = demand) and an efficient allocation of resources.

Classical economics was the dominant ideological structure of economics through much of the 19th century, until the Great Depression of the 1930s and the emergence of Keynesian economics. It also shares similarities with later neoclassical economics, which also stresses the importance of free markets.

ADAM SMITH AND
THE WEALTH OF NATIONS

Published in the same year as the U.S. Declaration of Independence (1776), *The Wealth of Nations* was suitably revolutionary in formalizing many economic ideas to help explain the new world of trade, commerce and industry.

The British philosopher Adam Smith (1723–90) was a leading critic of mercantilism, arguing that free trade would increase economic welfare. Smith helped to formalize ideas such as the free market and the "invisible hand" — Smith coined the latter phrase to explain how the pursuit of selfish interests would cause markets to adjust and provide for the common good.

▲ *British philosopher Adam Smith.*

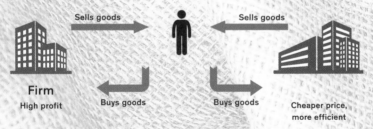

Sells goods   Sells goods

Firm
High profit   Buys goods   Buys goods   Cheaper price, more efficient

▲ *The invisible hand = self-interest + competitive marketplace. In this case, the high profit made by one firm encourages a new firm to enter the market, selling at a lower price. If markets are competitive, then the invisible hand helps to prevent firms making excess profits.*

> ...he intends only his own gain, and he is in this, as in many other cases, led by an invisible hand to promote an end which was no part of his intention... Pursuing his own interest he frequently promotes that of the society more effectually than when he really intends to promote it.
>
> Adam Smith, *The Wealth of Nations*

Adam Smith also developed theories of specialization and division of labor that were very important in the Industrial Revolution. Less well known is the fact that Adam Smith was nonetheless wary of capitalists, especially those who had monopoly power (see page 110). But Smith wasn't a libertarian — he believed there was a role for the government in providing public goods, the protection of private property and the regulation of monopoly.

The Wealth of Nations was important in helping to formalize the discipline of economics and providing the cornerstone of a classical economics broadly supportive of free markets. It is still referred to — and still a source of debate — even 250 years later.

HOW DOES ACTING IN YOUR OWN SELF-INTEREST LEAD TO THE COMMON GOOD?

Companies want to make profits.

Companies produce goods that people want.

High profits attract new companies to produce cheaper goods.

Consumers benefit from lower prices.

Buying the goods you want provides employment for other people.

◀ *A statue of philosopher Adam Smith, outside St. Giles Cathedral in Edinburgh.*

MARXISM

Marxism turned classical economics on its head. Rather than advocate private ownership and leave things to the free market, under Marxism the state would abolish private property and keep the means of production (e.g., factories) under common ownership. According to Marxism, this would enable a fair distribution of a nation's wealth. Marxism developed out of the Industrial Revolution, which saw a dramatic growth in inequality, with owners of capital gaining wealth, but workers remaining on low pay in very difficult conditions.

▲ German philosopher Karl Marx.

Karl Marx (1818–83), a German-born philosopher who spent much of his life in London, argued that the inequality of capitalism would inevitably cause the oppressed workers (the so-called proletariat) to revolt and, after subsequent repetitions of this process, create a classless communist society based on equality and shared ownership.

Marx's predictions proved ill-founded. The most advanced capitalist societies began to regulate capitalism, improving

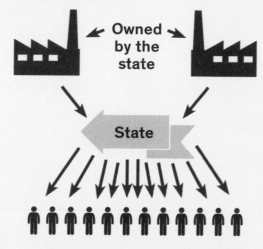

▲ Under Marxism, the state owns the means of production and decides what to produce. The state then decides how to distribute goods to the population.

leading to shortages and surpluses. In communist economies, production was centrally managed. If there was a shortage of goods (like bread), firms were not free to increase price and shift production from, for example, guns to bread. The shortage of bread continued until bureaucratic decisions were changed.

working conditions and increasing the real wages (wages adjusted for inflation) of workers. Rather than seek a communist revolution, workers were more likely to aspire to better-paid jobs and the hope of joining the growing middle class. Countries that did experience revolution found themselves in the hands of corrupt or over-powerful governments.

In economic terms, the problem with Marx's utopian ideal was that equal pay and the absence of incentives meant that communist economies tended to become stagnant and inefficient,

However, Marxist thought was the inspiration behind the Russian Revolution, and socialist critiques of the worst excesses of capitalism remained a potent ideological force throughout the 20th century. The fall of the Berlin Wall in 1989 seemed to suggest the irrevocable defeat of Marx's vision, though his questioning of the fairness of capitalism remains pertinent.

KEYNESIAN REVOLUTION

The essential idea of the British economist John Maynard Keynes (1883–1946) was that government intervention can prevent the worst excesses of the economic cycle (the natural fluctuation between expansion growth and recession — boom and bust) and provide relief from mass unemployment. (See Economic Cycle, page 182.)

Until the 1930s, classical free-market economics was the prevailing orthodoxy in most Western economies. However, the Great Depression, which originated in the United States and had a global impact, provided a clear challenge to the faith in unregulated free markets. Classical economics suggested that markets would clear and any disequilibrium (unemployment) would be short-lived. But the mass unemployment of the Great Depression made this theory look impractical or, at worst, counterproductive.

Keynes argued that markets didn't always clear. Wages in particular can be sticky downward (workers resist nominal wage cuts), causing unemployment. Also, in a recession people become pessimistic about the future, spending less and saving more (see Paradox of Thrift, page 126). Therefore, in a recession an

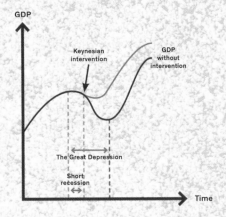

▲ *The Great Depression led to a prolonged fall in economic output. The aim of Keynesian intervention is to avoid this and achieve a quick economic recovery.*

economy can suffer from insufficient demand and this cycle of depressed demand can be hard to break.

> Economists set themselves too easy, too useless a task, if in tempestuous seasons they can only tell us, that when the storm is long past, the ocean is flat again.
>
> J.M. Keynes, *A Tract on Monetary Reform*

"IN THE LONG RUN WE ARE ALL DEAD"

Faced with mass unemployment, classical economists maintained that markets would clear in the long run. But, Keynes asked, why wait for the long run when we will be dead by the time the markets clear? Keynes wanted action now, not hope that in a few years things would be better. Keynes believed the government could speed up recovery by borrowing from the private sector (which had surplus savings) and investing in the economy. He argued that this injection into the economy could break the cycle of depression, deflation and high unemployment.

The *General Theory of Employment, Interest and Money* (1936) was revolutionary, creating a whole new branch of economics that examined how governments could influence the economic cycle. But it was also controversial, because it overturned many economic orthodoxies, such as balanced budgets (no borrowing) and limited government intervention.

NEO-KEYNESIANISM

After the Second World War, Keynes' ideas were popularized by the American economist Paul Samuelson, whose 1948 textbook *Economics* attempted to explain Keynesian ideas using more orthodox methods. In fact, it so simplified Keynesianism that in 1962 the British economist Joan Robinson criticized this orthodox-Keynesian synthesis as "Bastard Keynesianism." Nonetheless, Keynesianism — or what became known as neo-Keynesianism — was influential in the post-war Western world, at least until the stagflation of the 1970s, when it was challenged by a revival of more classical ideas. The 1970s was a difficult time for Keynesian theory because standard Keynesian policies of fiscal policy struggled to deal with both higher unemployment and higher inflation.

MONETARISM

Monetarism stresses the importance of regulating inflation by controlling the money supply. It was developed by the American economist Milton Friedman (1912–2006) and challenged many tenets of Keynesianism.

The basic theory of monetarism is that if the money supply increases faster than national output, the result will be inflation. Monetarists advocate monetary policy to control the growth of the money supply and keep inflation under check. In explaining the Great Depression, monetarists argued that deflation and prolonged unemployment were caused by the failure of a central bank to sufficiently support the money supply during a major recession (see Independent Central Banks, page 230).

Monetarism was a rather obscure branch of economics until the stagflation of the 1970s. But the combination of recession and inflation seemed to break the post-war Keynesian consensus and allowed the new radical ideas of monetarism to be tried in the United States. and the United Kingdom. As well as controlling inflation, monetarism has become associated with free-market

> Inflation is always and everywhere a monetary phenomenon.
>
> Milton Friedman,
> *Inflation Causes and Consequences*

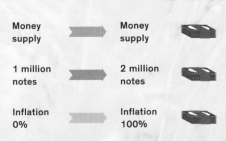

Money supply		Money supply	
1 million notes		2 million notes	
Inflation 0%		Inflation 100%	

▲ *Initially, the money supply is 1 million notes and inflation is 0 percent. If the money supply is doubled to 2 million notes, there will be inflation of 100 percent.*

economics and the belief in supply-side economics, which stress deregulation of the economy and less government intervention.

In 1979, U.S. Federal Reserve Chairman Paul Volcker pursued a form of monetarism, seeking to control inflation by limiting the growth of the money supply according to Friedman's rule. Under Volcker, interest rates were increased to an astonishing 20 percent in 1981. Volcker was successful in reducing inflation (caused by the legacy of 1970s cost-push inflation), which peaked at 14 percent in 1980, but fell to 3 percent in 1983. However, although inflation was reduced, it was at the high cost of a double-dip recession and unemployment rising to 10 percent.

Supporters of monetarism believe that this was a necessary consequence of bringing inflation under control. Critics of monetarism argue that the link between the money supply and inflation is weaker than Friedman claimed, and that the deflationary policies were unnecessarily harsh. Today, most central banks target inflation directly, rather than indirectly through the money supply. Nonetheless, Friedman's work has made a major contribution to the operation of monetary policy (see Monetary Policy, page 210).

▲ *Milton Friedman. Nobel Prize–winning economist and leading monetarist.*

MIXED ECONOMIES

For much of the 20th century, economics has been framed as a debate between free-market economics and socialism (or social democracy). In practice, economics is usually something of a pragmatic fudge. Even economies considered to be capitalist are in practice mixed economies — a combination of government intervention and free markets.

MIXED ECONOMIES — THE BEST OF BOTH WORLDS

Private goods are left to the private sector and the invisible hand helps to promote the goods people want. Public goods such as health care and education are usually provided in some measure by the government because the profit motive isn't as effective here.

SYNTHESIS OF IDEOLOGIES

In economic circles, the distinctions between different theories like Keynesianism and monetarism are not always clear-cut (especially since the 2008 financial crisis — see Credit Crunch, page 266). Theories are constantly evolving, reacting to new events and incorporating new ideas. And although economists may fall into camps such as Keynesian or monetarist, they will be open to adopting elements of different schools of thought. Furthermore, some economists believe these traditional economic distinctions don't address the real economic issues, and that we should consider issues like the environment, quality of life and development economics.

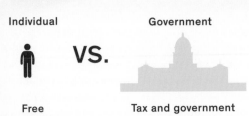

Individual

VS.

Government

Free market

Tax and government spending

◀ *In a mixed economy we try to combine the best of free markets and government intervention. Sometimes it is best to leave decisions to individuals, but sometimes government can improve economic welfare.*

Recent years have seen a growth in new economic ideas:

BEHAVIORAL ECONOMICS looks at economics through complex mechanisms of human psychology. Sometimes as individuals we are risk averse, for example, taking out holiday or life insurance. Other times we like to gamble, playing the lottery or placing bets. Behavioral economics looks at the contradictions and paradoxes in human nature.

ENVIRONMENTAL ECONOMICS is concerned with the use of natural resources and how economic activity impacts the environment. It is also concerned with policies and incentives that can try to harmonize economic activity with environmental issues. For example, carbon tax to reduce the impact of global warming. Environmental economics often prioritizes environmental sustainability above gross domestic product (GDP).

HAPPINESS ECONOMICS considers factors that affect happiness and quality of life. With an understanding of what causes happiness, economists can make suggestions for how economic policy can improve the quality of life. Happiness economics expands the scope of economics from maximizing monetary values to considering issues such as civil liberties, health and leisure. Happiness economics often prioritizes welfare above GDP.

DEVELOPMENT ECONOMICS is concerned with improving living standards and welfare in low-income countries. It aims to reduce global economic inequality. Development economics investigates policies for economic growth, structural change and long-term development. It includes a wider range of political and social policies than traditional economics.

ECONOMICS — SCIENCE OR ART?

Economists collect data, create models, develop theories, suggest policies and even make predictions, but is the subject of economics a science or art? Some aspects of economics, like mathematical models, are a form of scientific analysis, but the use of economic data tends to be very much an art — just look at how the same economic data can be presented in so many different ways.

Economics combines positive science (data) and normative science (data presented in a certain way) with judgments on policy. For example, looking at data on net migration levels, the economist can suggest why these levels occurred, and use models and theories to predict the impact on wages and economic growth. Using the same data, some economists may emphasize how immigration boosts GDP, while other economists may emphasize how it can depress wages for low-skilled workers.

Economists start with science and data, but the conclusions they reach can be highly subjective because there are many possible variables, and how they are interpreted can depend on the preferences of the economist.

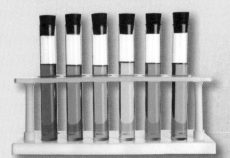

An economist is an expert who will know tomorrow why the things he predicted yesterday didn't happen today.

Laurence J. Peter

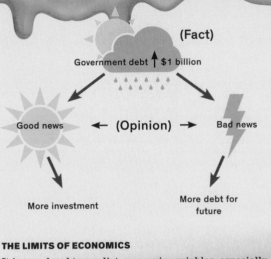

(Fact)

Government debt ↑ $1 billion

Good news ← **(Opinion)** → Bad news

More investment

More debt for future

◀ *Government debt increased $1 billion. We could view this as good news for the economy (more borrowing enables more investment and higher growth) or we could view this as bad news for the economy (more debt for future generations).*

THE LIMITS OF ECONOMICS

It is very hard to predict economic variables, especially far into the future. One aspect of economics is that you can end up with different interpretations of the same data. Higher debt may be seen by one economist as a good thing, but by another economist as not so good! This uncertainty of outcomes is a common refrain in economics. It can be frustrating for those who like mathematical certainty, but this is the real economic world — full of unpredictable events and the irrational behavior of individuals.

CHAPTER 1

MARKETS

SUPPLY AND DEMAND

Even non-economists cannot escape the ubiquity of supply and demand. If you try to buy even a small apartment in an exclusive district of Manhattan or London, you won't get much change from a million dollars or pounds. Why is it so expensive? It is the operation of supply and demand.

Demand shows the price people are willing to pay for a good. As price rises, demand usually falls.

Supply is the quantity of goods firms are willing to offer on the market. As price rises, firms typically want to sell more because it is more profitable.

WHY HOUSING CAN BE SO EXPENSIVE

Essentially, demand for housing is very high in Manhattan and London because there are many highly paid jobs in those cities. But the supply of housing is very limited because it is difficult to find the space to

▶ In Manhattan the price of an apartment can exceed $1 million. This is due to very limited supply, but high demand. The Midwest, in contrast, has less demand, more supply and therefore cheaper prices.

build new houses. So there are a lot of highly paid workers competing for a limited quantity of housing. The relative shortage of supply means that as demand rises, prices increase.

In the U.S. Midwest during the 19th century, settlers had the freedom to build their own house on vast tracts of land. The value of a house was about equal to the cost of the building materials. There was no shortage — supply of housing could easily increase with demand. But modern New York and London are very different.

$1 million $1,000

Millions of people

3 people

▲ As demand for housing rises in highly populated areas, prices increase. In areas with more land available, there is no shortage of housing and this keeps prices down.

CHARGING A HIGH PRICE IF YOU CAN
In the 1800s, the French Emperor Napoleon approached a hotel on the slopes of Col du Pin Bouchain. Napoleon was shocked at the price of eggs, and so he asked the owner of the hotel:

"Are eggs so rare in this region that they justify such a bill?" The owner of the hotel replied, "It's not the eggs that are rare, it's emperors."

The hotel owner was aware that the Emperor had the capacity to pay a high price, and he had control over the sale of eggs in that area (see Monopoly, page 110). He also had a lot of courage to ask Napoleon to pay such a price!

THE INVISIBLE HAND

As we have seen, Adam Smith's concept of the invisible hand suggests that individual agents acting in their own self-interest will cause equilibrium in markets. How does this happen? There is no one who sits down and sets the global price of cappuccinos, so what determines the average market price?

▲ When the price is $1.20, the demand for coffee is greater than supply — this leads to queues in coffee shops. Firms will respond by raising prices. Prices will rise to $2.00, where supply = demand.

Suppose you open a coffee shop and start selling very good coffee for $1. You are likely to enjoy a full café, with queues of people waiting to get a seat and buy a coffee. There will be a shortage of seats — and demand will be greater than supply. As the café owner, these queues of customers will give you an incentive to increase the price. Even with a higher price, you will still fill the café, but now you will get more revenue. You should increase the price until equilibrium is reached and there are no more queues of

people — until the higher price reduces some of the demand. But if you set up a coffee shop and try to charge $10 (even for very good coffee), you would get very few customers and be left with lots of unsold coffee. In this case, the answer is to reduce the price and attract more customers.

INCENTIVES AND THE INVISIBLE HAND

The invisible hand can also help to distribute resources to where demand is greatest.

Suppose a company starts selling a new product like organic kale. If it becomes a fashionable food item, the company can charge a high price and make a high profit. However, if the company makes a high profit, it acts as an incentive for other companies to enter the market and produce and sell organic kale. Eventually, supply will increase and reduce the price.

> The reason that the invisible hand often seems invisible is that it is often not there.
>
> Joseph E. Stiglitz, *Making Globalization Work*

THE INVISIBLE HAND IS SOMETIMES NOT THERE

Adam Smith's concept of the "invisible hand" may have endured, but that doesn't mean that it is always in operation.

For example, if a company has very strong brand loyalty, it may be able to keep increasing the price of its goods because the goods produced by rivals are not considered by consumers to be acceptable substitutes. So the latest-model iPhone sells for hundreds of dollars, enabling Apple to maintain a very large profit margin.

The price of a newly released iPhone reflects the brand loyalty that some consumers feel toward Apple. In this case, there is no invisible hand pushing down the price.

UNDERGROUND MARKETS

Sometimes you hear of concert tickets going for very high prices on secondary (or underground) markets. In 2016 a ticket for an Adele concert in London sold for £24,840 (around US$32,000) — 299 times the original price of £83 (US$107). This can also be explained by supply and demand.

Most fans who buy a ticket are not interested in reselling it for profit, and just want to see the concert. Therefore, very few people are willing to sell tickets on the secondary market, and the supply of these "extra" tickets will be very limited. However, because thousands of people want to see the concert, there are likely to be some very rich people both willing and able to pay astronomical prices. The irony is that because ticket scalping is illegal, it can increase prices on the underground market. The fewer people who take the risk to sell, the more limited supply is, and the higher the price will be.

PARADOX OF THE WAR ON DRUGS

It is the same with illegal drugs. By targeting production and destroying illegal drugs where they are grown, supply is reduced and prices may be pushed up. In other words, the harder governments work to limit supply, the relatively more profitable (and therefore tempting) it is to become a drug dealer.

The paradox is that it seems to be a good idea to destroy drug supplies. One argument put forward for legalizing drugs is that it would put many criminals out of business because drug dealing would no longer be profitable on the underground market (though of course there are many other issues at stake).

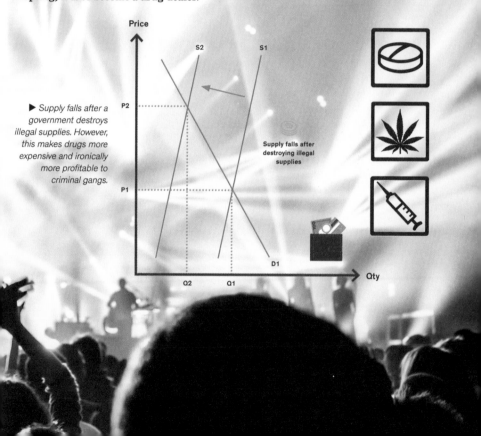

▶ *Supply falls after a government destroys illegal supplies. However, this makes drugs more expensive and ironically more profitable to criminal gangs.*

Supply falls after destroying illegal supplies

UTILITY MAXIMIZATION

Economic theory assumes that individuals seek to maximize their personal utility — that is, their satisfaction and happiness. In simple terms, you buy the goods that you want or need the most.

MARGINAL SATISFACTION

An important concept is that we make decisions at the margin. Or put another way — does the second piece of cake make you happy?

One piece of cake may give you a lot of satisfaction (have a high marginal utility), and you may be willing to pay $5 for a single piece. But just because you like cake, it doesn't mean you will gain as much satisfaction from a second piece on the same visit to the café. The marginal utility of a second piece of cake is much less than that of the first. If a second piece

of cake costs $5, but you think it will give you only $1 of utility, you're likely to leave it for another, hungrier day.

In theory, consumers will evaluate the marginal utility (the satisfaction they

> ## UTILITARIANISM
>
> • • • • • • •
>
> The philosophy that we should seek to maximize the happiness of the greatest number of people

High utility

Less utility

Starting to feel unwell

◀ *The marginal utility of a second or third piece of cake is much less than that of the first.*

BUDGET CONSTRAINTS AND UTILITY

We could make a link between utility maximization and our evolutionary development. When a caveman made a decision to go hunting, he was evaluating whether this was the best use of his time and energy. A successful hunter could then barter some of his meat for a better axe. This bartering was a way to maximize his utility. If he made irrational decisions, such as not keeping a safe place to live, it could be the difference between survival or death.

Fortunately, in an era of relative abundance, our utility maximization is less often about survival and more about maximizing our happiness given the variety of choices.

think they will derive) of each unit of consumption. If the utility is equal to or greater than the cost of that unit, then they will buy.

PARADOX OF VALUE

The prices of goods don't always reflect their usefulness to society. Water is essential, but cheap. Diamonds are mere ornaments, but command a very high price. So why are we willing to pay a high price for diamonds but only a low price for water?

One reason is that we buy very few diamonds in our lifetime. The marginal utility of one diamond ring in a lifetime is very high. We are willing to pay a lot for an engagement ring. But, once we have bought our partner one diamond ring, we will (hopefully) never buy another!

Of course, some people may like buying diamonds every year, but for many it is a once-in-a-lifetime purchase. But many people buy water every day. The marginal utility of water doesn't diminish as we get older, because we still need it just as much as we did the first time we bought it. Over our lifetimes, we probably end up spending more in total on water than we do on diamonds, even though the actual unit price is very different.

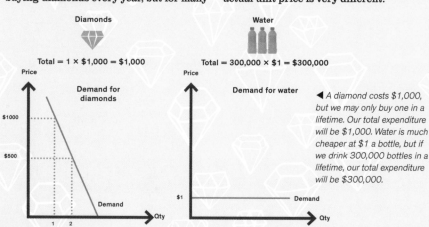

Diamonds

Total = 1 × $1,000 = $1,000

Water

Total = 300,000 × $1 = $300,000

◀ *A diamond costs $1,000, but we may only buy one in a lifetime. Our total expenditure will be $1,000. Water is much cheaper at $1 a bottle, but if we drink 300,000 bottles in a lifetime, our total expenditure will be $300,000.*

VALUE AND SCARCITY

The value of a product is also related to its scarcity. Diamond production has been controlled by a few large producers — restricting supply means that prices can be kept high. It is much harder to stop people from entering the market for water supply if the profits are high.

"MY KINGDOM FOR A BOTTLE OF WATER"

With apologies to Shakespeare, suppose you were in a desert, very thirsty and miles from anywhere. Would you spend your last dollar on a diamond or a bottle of water? You would buy the water of course. In this scenario, the marginal utility of water is clearly greater than that of a diamond. All the diamonds in the world would suddenly lose any appeal if you were dying from thirst. If there was only one bottle of water for sale, you may be willing to spend your entire wealth on it to stay alive.

Going back to Shakespeare, we can now understand in economic terms why King Richard III would give up his kingdom for the temporary loan of a horse, because he realizes that the marginal utility of fleeing from battle and capture (and death) is the only thing that matters at that moment. It shows how the marginal utility of products can change very quickly.

IRRATIONAL BEHAVIOR

The theory of marginal utility is neat, but how well does it relate to the real world? When you go shopping, do you weigh up the marginal utility and marginal cost of products? I don't think many people stand in a supermarket aisle weighing up the marginal utility of a bunch of bananas (not even economists). In the real world, there are many factors other than marginal utility that influence consumption.

BOUNDED RATIONALITY

This idea suggests people are rational, but, due to an excess of choices, we take shortcuts that may be suboptimal. For example, buying out of habit. We buy the same cereal for breakfast because we don't have the time to evaluate every cereal on the market. If we could try them all, we may find a new cereal that is marginally better — but is it worth the effort? Speed and making do with what we know will work is important.

IMPULSE BUYING

Sometimes we buy things that are "conveniently" placed (by clever retailers) at the checkout. They are put there very deliberately to encourage impulse buying — usually highly profitable items, like chocolate, or gimmicky things, like portable fans on hot days. This impulse buying is an aspect of human nature: sometimes we waste money because, well, it seemed like a good idea at the time.

HERDING BEHAVIOR

Individuals may respond to collective actions of a group rather than evaluate the individual merits of the case. For example, if house prices are rising, and the majority of participants in the housing market believe prices will keep rising, it is tempting to assume the majority view must be correct. This is known as the "wisdom of the crowds." It can be difficult to challenge the conventional viewpoint.

LACK OF SELF-CONTROL

From a rational perspective, we can devise a study plan to spend two hours revising for our exams in the early evening. However, before we know it, it is midnight and we have spent hours surfing the internet. From a long-term perspective, it is irrational to waste time, but through lack of discipline and effort we get caught up in suboptimal choices. If we go on a diet, but have no self-control, we are bound to fail.

ALTRUISM

• • •

Altruism involves people considering the welfare of other people, e.g., giving to charity or employing a worker to save them from unemployment. Orthodox economics usually assumes we are self-serving — trying to maximize our personal utility or wealth. However, this ignores genuine altruism — where we give to others without any expectation of something in return. The motivation for altruism is harder to measure because it is not as simple as profit maximization.

OPTIMISM BIAS

• • • • • • • •

This occurs when people believe they are less at risk of a negative event than the average person. For example, people may underestimate their chances of becoming ill, so they don't take out health insurance or make a will. The optimism bias of financial traders can lead to a bubble in share prices because traders continue to buy and hold, thinking they will be able to get out of the bubble, just in time; they assume they can beat the market.

VEBLEN GOODS

For some types of goods, a low price indicates low status and people don't value it. A higher price indicates better status and makes the good more attractive for those who wish to display their social status.

If goods become more expensive, they become more exclusive. If you can afford to buy and display these exclusive goods, you can signal to the rest of society that you are successful and perhaps even a member of the top 1 percent of society. Obvious examples of Veblen goods are fine art, luxury cars, expensive jewelry and haute couture clothes.

Veblen also used the term "conspicuous consumption" to explain the desire to own exclusive goods. For many people, buying Veblen goods is irrational, because the price is much greater than

Thorstein Veblen (1857–1929) was a Norwegian-American economist and sociologist. His best-known book is *The Theory of the Leisure Class* (1899), which criticized the "leisure class" and those who spent money on luxuries for the purpose of social display.

the utility. However, for some people the utility of Veblen goods comes from the prestige and sense of social position that these expensive goods convey.

When it comes to fine art, we may not know very much about the subject. But if the seller sets a high price, we may assume that it is of high quality.

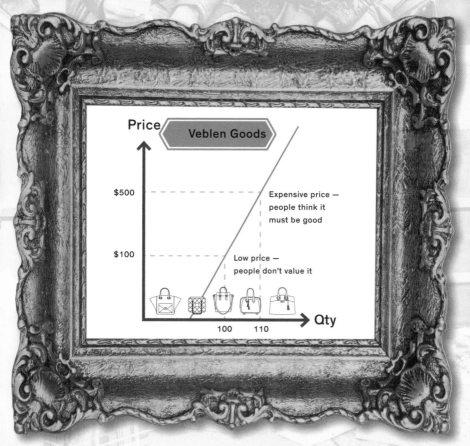

▲ *Veblen goods — a rare circumstance where a higher-priced good leads to higher demand.*

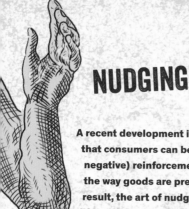

NUDGING

A recent development in economics is the idea of "nudges." This is the theory that consumers can be influenced by small suggestions and positive (or negative) reinforcements. Analysts have observed that a small change in the way goods are presented will strongly affect our buying decisions. As a result, the art of nudging has become a ubiquitous phenomenon in everyday life — "Would you like fries with that?"

If you go into a coffee shop and order a coffee, a good barista will ask a follow-up question: "Would you like a muffin to go with that?" Why are they trained to offer secondary choices? The simple reason is that we are much more likely to buy a muffin if it is directly offered as a choice. Perhaps you hadn't even thought of buying something to eat, but when you are asked whether you would like a tasty muffin, you think … Well, actually I do quite like muffins, thanks for the suggestion.

This kind of commercial nudge is especially successful in making us buy more food. You could argue that the widespread influence of nudging is one reason for the growth in obesity in the Western world. Everywhere firms try to sell us supersized drinks and fries, second portions and an extra dessert. Retailers know that it is difficult to turn down these nudges.

POSITIVE NUDGES

Nudging can work both ways, however, and there have been efforts by government and local authorities to nudge us toward healthier options. For example, retailers may be forced to display the number of calories prominently on the muffin you didn't know you wanted. We are offered the muffin. We say yes, then we read it has 450 calories! Maybe not, thank you!

Nudges can be as simple as sending encouraging messages. A study found that if students were sent encouraging text messages about their college progress, their attendance rates were higher. This is the positive reinforcement of nudging. However, although nudging can be used by schools and government to promote healthy eating and better spending habits, we face a very sophisticated commercial sector that tries to push products we don't necessarily need or want.

It is like a battle of the nudges: companies push high-sugar "energy drinks" by associating them with sporting celebrities to give the impression that they are a healthy choice; at the same time, health pressure groups try to discourage us from buying sugary drinks by linking them to obesity.

WHAT ARE SOME OF THE BEST TRICKS AND NUDGES?

SPECIAL INTRODUCTORY DEALS

If you get a new mobile phone contract, the first six months is often at a discounted rate, and it is this cheap monthly fee that is prominently displayed. But the smaller print reveals that, after the first six months, the average monthly rate doubles. The cheap introductory rate draws us in, and then we end up paying more.

In the mortgage boom of 2000, for example, new mortgages were offered with very low introductory rates, but after two years, monthly payments suddenly shot up and people found they were locked into the higher charges.

BARRIERS TO CANCELLATION

Companies make it easy to subscribe to extra services. However, once signed up, it can be difficult to cancel. Quite often they insist you phone customer services to request a cancellation. On the phone, customer services can then make an offer to try to make you stay.

OPPORTUNITY COST

Opportunity cost is the idea that gaining one item means we have to give up something else. The opportunity cost of spending your student loan on going out to parties is that you cannot spend this money on rent and textbooks. With limited resources, we have to make choices — we face opportunity costs.

Around election time, politicians will be keen to promise "No new taxes." But politicians, for obvious reasons, are not keen on highlighting the opportunity costs of their decisions. If there are "No new taxes," the opportunity costs could be higher levels of government borrowing or spending cuts to health care. However, this is usually left up to voters to work out for themselves — opportunity cost is often the cost you do not see.

If people are rational, they will weigh up the opportunity costs of their decisions. If we spend all day sleeping and watching TV, the opportunity cost is that we don't have time to study. But, of course, humans can be irrational and ignore or undervalue the opportunity cost — especially if it is to be paid in the future. Would you sacrifice going to a party in order to study for exams? The opportunity cost of one party is potentially a failed exam and worse job prospects. But sometimes the immediate present seems much more important than the distant future.

> The first lesson of economics is scarcity: There is never enough of anything to satisfy all those who want it. The first lesson of politics is to disregard the first lesson of economics.
>
> American economist Thomas Sowell, *Is Reality Optional? And Other Essays*, 1993

A good way of thinking about opportunity cost is to imagine a pie chart. If a government wants to increase spending on health care, the opportunity cost is that the money for the extra spending will have to come from elsewhere — the private sector, education, military spending and so on.

Government health care

Private sector

to reduce prices: by removing "frills" — free extras like meals — and drinks and gift bags, making it easy to charge less and limit availability.

The airline's opportunity cost of very cheap airline tickets makes it easier for them to compromise their customer service. For example, budget airlines may charge you for printing out your ticket at an airport.

NO SUCH THING AS A FREE LUNCH?

This is a well-known saying and it is related to the concept of opportunity cost. Suppose an airline gives you a "free meal" — is it really free? No! The airline will include the cost in the price of your ticket. And this is how budget airlines were able

A FREE GOOD

There are exceptions to this rule of opportunity cost. Some goods really can be "free" in all senses of the word. If you live in California, once you have put a solar panel on your roof, you can take the energy of the sun without any opportunity cost. If you live by Lake Michigan, there is no opportunity cost in taking a glass of water.

But while water for residents near Lake Michigan is a free good without opportunity cost, if you move back to California, water is more scarce and there is greater opportunity cost. If you water your garden in drought areas it can mean your neighbors don't have access to water.

> ## OPPORTUNITY COST AND ACTUAL COST
>
> • • • • • •
>
> Suppose you buy a new car for $10,000. After three years, it has depreciated in value to $3,000. What is the opportunity cost of deciding to keep the car? The opportunity cost of keeping the car is the $3,000 you could have got for selling the car. The price you bought it for is not relevant here.

ELASTICITY OF DEMAND

A fundamental law of economics states that higher prices will lead to lower demand. But by how much will demand fall? This is what elasticity measures — the responsiveness of demand to a change in price or income.

For example, if the price of electricity increases by 20 percent, we may notice a 2 percent fall in demand as some households limit non-essential use. We say that the demand for electricity is price inelastic — a change in price causes a smaller percentage change in demand. But if the price of low-quality sausages increases by 20 percent, we may notice a much larger 50 percent fall in demand as customers switch to alternative food items. In this case, we say that demand for sausages is price elastic — a change in price causes a bigger percentage change in demand.

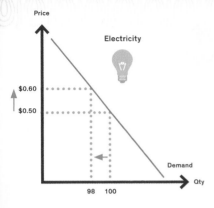

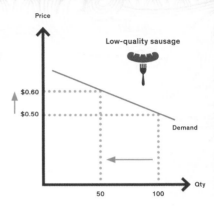

▲ *Electricity is price inelastic and demand is mostly unaffected by price rises. Higher prices for low-quality sausage means a fall in demand as customers buy alternative brands.*

IMPORTANCE OF ELASTICITY

• • • • • • • • • • • • • •

In the case of electricity, increasing the price is good for the producers, but not so good for consumers:

Initially, revenue is 100 million units at $0.50 per unit = $50 million.

After a 20 percent price increase, quantity drops by 2 percent to 98 million units at $0.60 per unit = $58.8 million.

Revenue therefore has increased by $8.8 million.

But in the case of low-quality sausages, the increase in price leads to a fall in revenue.

Initially, revenue is 100 million units at $0.50 per unit = $50 million.

After a 20 percent price increase, quantity drops by 50 percent to 50 million units at $0.60 per unit = $30 million.

Revenue therefore has decreased by $20 million.

Therefore, companies have an incentive to increase prices if they know demand is price inelastic. This is why prices tend to be higher in markets where firms have monopoly power.

WHY ARE SOME GOODS SENSITIVE TO PRICE?

Are there alternatives? If you are on an eight-hour train journey, there is only one place to buy a sandwich. If the cheapest sandwich is $8.00, you either buy it or go hungry. If prices are very high, it may encourage customers to buy in advance. But there will always be some who forget, and once on the train they are captive customers. Therefore, prices on trains are more inelastic than in city centers, where there are many more alternatives.

Is it a necessity? If the price of electricity goes up, you are unlikely to stop cooking. True, you could buy a gas oven, but that is a dramatic response to higher electricity prices. There is no real alternative to electricity, so demand is more price inelastic. But if the price of going on holiday to a particular country increases, there are alternatives, so price is more sensitive — or you may decide not to go on vacation this year.

Demand for cigarettes is very price inelastic because many smokers are addicted. This is why governments have often increased tax on cigarettes — it is an easy way to increase revenue as demand is inelastic in the short term.

If companies can increase revenue on inelastic goods, why don't they increase the price of chocolate, coffee and cigarettes?

Chocolate is price inelastic — there are not many close substitutes and it is often seen as a necessity! Therefore, if chocolate

producers increase the price of chocolate they would make more revenue. So why don't prices continually increase?

If the price of all chocolate increased, demand would be inelastic. But if one chocolate producer increases the prices of its chocolate bars, people simply switch to another producer's brands. Individual brands of demand-inelastic goods like coffee and chocolate, are very price sensitive; however, if all chocolate went up in price (such as in a shortage), the demand would become elastic.

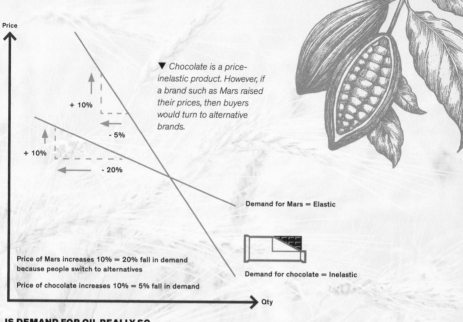

Price

▼ *Chocolate is a price-inelastic product. However, if a brand such as Mars raised their prices, then buyers would turn to alternative brands.*

+ 10%

- 5%

+ 10%

- 20%

Demand for Mars = Elastic

Price of Mars increases 10% = 20% fall in demand because people switch to alternatives

Price of chocolate increases 10% = 5% fall in demand

Demand for chocolate = Inelastic

Qty

IS DEMAND FOR OIL REALLY SO PRICE INELASTIC?

In the 1970s, the price of oil tripled overnight. Yet demand didn't fall very much. It was a classic example of inelastic demand. People with cars had no alternative but to keep buying gas. However, over time the story was different.

The higher price of oil was a shock to carmakers. Previously, it didn't matter if cars were "gas guzzlers." But now, in an era of high oil prices, fuel efficiency became a stronger selling point. The higher price encouraged greater fuel efficiency and different driving habits. A prolonged period of high oil prices may even encourage some people to find alternatives to cars. During the high oil prices of 2008/09, the United States and Europe saw an increase in alternative forms of transport, such as the bicycle.

The important thing is that in the short term demand is very inelastic. But, over time, people adapt to higher prices and try to find ways to develop alternatives.

INFERIOR GOODS

An inferior good is something you buy less of as your income rises. This may sound counterintuitive. If you have higher income, you can afford to buy more goods, and for most goods this will be the case — rising income means you buy more (these are called normal goods).

WHY WOULD HIGHER INCOME CAUSE YOU TO BUY LESS OF SOME GOODS?

Suppose you have to shop on a tight budget, so you buy the cheapest bread you can find. But if your income increases, you may want to buy better-quality bread — rather than getting a $1 loaf, you might feel wealthy enough to treat yourself to an organic loaf that costs $5. Income elasticity of demand measures how a change in income affects demand for goods. If your income increases, you can afford to buy more goods. But will you actually buy more?

TRAVEL

Another good example of an inferior good is bus travel. Generally, bus travel between cities is the cheapest form of transport, but it is also the slowest and most uncomfortable. Because it is an inferior good, bus travel is likely to be

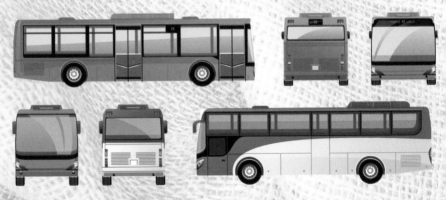

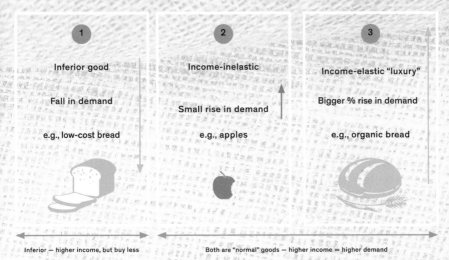

	1		2		3
	Inferior good		Income-inelastic		Income-elastic "luxury"
	Fall in demand		Small rise in demand		Bigger % rise in demand
	e.g., low-cost bread		e.g., apples		e.g., organic bread

Inferior — higher income, but buy less   Both are "normal" goods — higher income = higher demand

▲ *A rise in income has different effects for different types of goods. With an inferior good (low-cost bread), a consumer buys less because they can switch to "luxury" bread, e.g., organic multigrain.*

marketed at students and people with low incomes. When students gain a high-paying job, they are likely to stop using the bus and choose short-haul flights or high-speed train travel instead.

ECONOMIC GROWTH AND INFERIOR GOODS

In the post-war period, canned foods played an important role in people's diet. Canned foods are cheap, effective forms of nourishment. However, with economic growth and higher incomes, consumers have switched to fresh vegetables and meat rather than relying on canned meat (e.g., Spam).

In a recession, we tend to see a rise in demand for canned foods. Lower incomes mean there is an increased demand for these inferior goods (in favor of dining out at restaurants or purchasing fresh organic vegetables). In the 2009 recession, the United States saw an 11 percent rise in demand for canned goods. Interestingly, at the same time there was also a rise in demand for family planning and contraception. Perhaps in a recession, people prefer the small cost of contraception rather than the much bigger cost of feeding another child.

CHAPTER 2

MARKET
FAILURE

EXTERNALITIES

Market failure occurs when unregulated free markets cause inefficiency and fail to provide the optimal outcome. Congestion, bank runs, unemployment, pollution, artificially high prices — all are signs that the free market is failing to provide the most efficient outcome.

Externalities occur when producing or consuming a good has an impact on a third party. If you drive a car during peak time, you face the private costs of fuel, but you don't have to pay for the negative costs to other people, such as increased congestion and increased pollution.

The problem with externalities is that we don't usually consider them when making economic decisions. While enjoying a 450-calorie muffin, we don't take into account the possible negative externalities to the health care system for treating diabetes in the future.

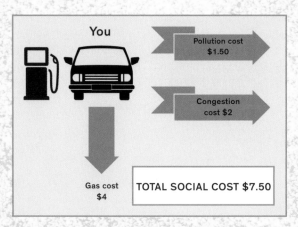

You

Pollution cost
$1.50

Congestion
cost $2

Gas cost
$4

TOTAL SOCIAL COST $7.50

◀ *Private cost is the cost you incure to fill up your car with gas. The external costs describe those faced by other people, e.g., more congestion, more pollution.*

OVERCONSUMPTION IN A FREE MARKET

Everybody wants to drive to work because it is cheaper, more convenient and you don't have to sit next to a stranger. But if everyone decides to drive to work in the morning, it can lead to traffic jams. This is a classic example of market failure, and everyone loses out because of the gridlock.

If you try to reduce traffic jams by taking the bus to work, it will make little difference. With just one car fewer on the road, you will still be stuck in a traffic jam, and now you will be sitting on a bus next to a stranger. For most people the rational decision is still to drive — at least you'll be more comfortable in the traffic jam. The problem is that individuals face only the private cost. They don't have to pay the full social cost — which is not just the private cost of fuel, but also the congestion and pollution costs of driving.

DEADWEIGHT WELFARE LOSS OF CONGESTION

This external cost of congestion causes deadweight welfare loss to society.

- Everyone wastes time taking longer to get to work.
- We spend more on gas sitting in traffic.
- Worsening of air quality.
- It may even deter us from traveling into a city center, so businesses can lose out as well.

"Capitalism is the astonishing belief that the nastiest motives of the nastiest men somehow or other work for the best results in the best of all possible worlds."

Attributed to
John Maynard Keynes

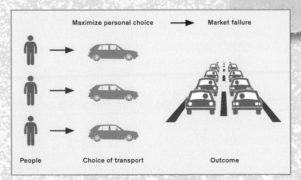

◀ To maximize personal welfare, individuals may choose to drive a car. However, if others also choose to drive to work, the outcome can lead to market failure (gridlock and congestion).

SOCIAL BENEFIT

· · · · · · · · ·

The social benefit of education includes the total benefit to society — the private benefit (higher-paying job for an individual), but the indirect external benefits to the economy include a better-educated workforce and a more informed political system.

Social benefit = private benefit + external benefits

POSITIVE EXTERNALITIES

Externalities can also be positive. If you choose to cycle into town, there is the positive benefit to everyone else of less pollution. If you have a vaccination against infectious disease, there is an obvious personal benefit, but your improved health can benefit others in society too.

UNDERPROVISION OF POSITIVE EXTERNALITIES

In the first half of the 19th century, provision of health care and education was very poor, with young children often working in factories. Education was underprovided because, although there were high private and external benefits, there was little incentive for poor families to make the sacrifice required to send children to school.

Education didn't just benefit children, but also provided companies with a more productive workforce. But in a free market, education was underprovided. It required state intervention to provide universal education for children. In the long term, society benefited from the improvements in education standards.

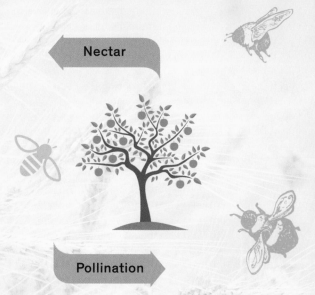

Nectar

▶ *Apple farmers provide positive externalities of blossom and nectar for beekeepers. Beekeepers provide a positive externality to apple farmers — their bees help to pollinate the apple tree. It is a mutually beneficial relationship.*

Pollination

SOCIAL EFFICIENCY

The free market can lead to a type of efficiency — producing goods for the lowest cost. Social efficiency requires taking into account the social benefit, social cost and all the externalities of consumption and production.

BEES AND APPLE TREES

This is a classic example of two complementary positive externalities. Bees provide a positive externality by fertilizing the nearby apple trees. The apple trees provide a positive externality by providing nectar for bees and in turn honey for the beekeeper. Bees are responsible for pollinating more than 400 agricultural plants, such as apples, avocados, blueberries, cucumber, kiwis and melons. Those who help preserve bee populations provide a very important positive externality for the food chain.

PUBLIC GOODS

Public goods benefit everyone in society, but in a free market they may not be provided at all. This is because you can enjoy the benefit of a public good without having to contribute toward its cost. Therefore, although socially beneficial, it may not be profitable for companies to provide them.

Examples of public goods include:
- National defense
- Cleaning up the environment
- Street lighting
- Law and order

FEATURES OF PUBLIC GOODS

If you consume a public good, it doesn't reduce the amount available to others (something known as non-rivalry). If you eat an apple, no one else can benefit — once eaten, it is gone. But if you walk under a street light, the light is still available for everyone else.

The second feature of public goods is that if you provide the good, you can't stop people benefiting from it. If you reduce crime by better policing, everyone in society benefits from a lower crime rate. If you provide street lighting, you have no option but to accept it will be lighter at night for everyone.

Private good   Public good

◀ An apple is limited, nobody else can eat it. If you walk under a street light, the light remains for many others to consume.

Free-rider problem

Because you can't prevent people from consuming public goods, in a free market, people can enjoy the good without paying for it. If you have a beautiful front garden, you can't charge people who walk past it.

This becomes an issue for public services, such as improving transit or maintaining a public garden. If you provide a network of street lights, people benefit from the light, but it is not practical to charge them for using the service. You could ask for contributions, but the individual may hope someone else pays for the good, which they can then enjoy without having to contribute. In other words, there is an incentive to "free-ride" on those who are willing to pay. Suppose there is a scheme to protect against flooding:

- The total cost is $20 million.
- Personal benefit is $100 per person.
- Population is 1 million.
- The net benefit to society is $100m.
- Thus the scheme has a large social benefit of $100 million compared to a cost of just $20 million.

To provide the scheme, you would need everyone to pay $20, which is less than the benefit they get of $100. However, would people volunteer the $20? There is a temptation to free-ride on the efforts of others. In a population of 1 million, you may decide to leave it up to others to pay. So a private company becomes reluctant to provide flood defenses because it is not sure that people will contribute to the cost.

COMPULSORY TAX

The free-rider problem is why public goods are generally paid for by compulsory taxes, which means you don't have the option of free-riding on others. The tax levied to pay for the flood-defense scheme would be $20 per person, but the community profits from the scheme because the total benefit is greater than the total cost.

FREE-RIDER PROBLEM

The free-rider problem is not just an issue with public goods. If you have ever been a student living in a house with a shared kitchen, you will probably have seen the free-rider problem in action. Many students will wait in the hope that someone else will clean the kitchen — they will benefit from a clean kitchen without having to do any work. The result is often a kitchen that goes uncleaned for quite a long time, as everyone holds out for someone else to do the dirty work.

PUBLIC GOODS AND LOCAL COMMUNITIES VS. BIG CITIES

• • • • • • • • • • • • • • • •

Suppose you have a small, tight-knit local community that wants to reduce crime in the area. The locals may meet up and agree to all contribute to a fund to employ a private security guard. People could free-ride on the efforts of others, but because they know everyone else and they want a reputation as good citizens, they are happy to pay. Therefore, in this local case, the public good can be provided by the free market and private citizens.

However, would this model work for a city of 5 million? All citizens would benefit from contributing to private security, but it is much easier to be anonymous among 5 million other people, and there isn't the same community spirit. If you free-ride on others, it's unlikely anyone will know. So the bigger the scale, the more challenging it is for the private sector to provide public goods.

SHOWROOMING AND THE FREE-RIDER PROBLEM

Showrooming is when we look at products in a store then go home and buy them online at a cheaper price. Many consumers like browsing in traditional bookstores — it gives them a much better sense of the book than an online photograph can. However, there is the temptation to browse in a bookstore and then go home and order the book online at the cheaper price.

If every consumer used the bookstore to browse but then bought online, the bookstore would close down. Store owners, then, must rely on the fact that some consumers will be willing to pay slightly higher prices, which will keep them in business. Some stores have

Bookstore
$12

Online bookstore
$10

◄ *A bookstore has a high cost of renting and higher prices for its books. An online bookstore has lower costs and can usually sell product for a cheaper price. However, always buying online may lead to the loss of real bookstores.*

considered charging people for trying on clothes, and then waiving this fee if they buy the clothes.

TAX HAVENS AND FREE-RIDING

Some multinational companies have successfully reduced their corporation tax bills by registering in countries with very low tax rates, such as the Bahamas and Liechtenstein, while operating in higher-tax economies. The companies benefit from the public spending of the governments (educated workforce, health care subsidies and infrastructure spending) in the countries in which they operate. But by paying no tax, they are free-riding on other workers and companies who do pay tax. They rely on others to pay tax so that they can benefit from public spending.

Companies who use tax havens will defend themselves by saying they indirectly pay tax, in the form of the income tax of employees and sales tax on the goods they sell. But by reducing the corporate tax burden there is an element of free-riding, especially online companies that avoid the local taxes paid by bricks-and-mortar businesses. If everyone was able to register in the Bahamas, the governments would have to cut spending or find other ways to collect tax.

TRAGEDY OF THE COMMONS

This is where individual users share a common resource, but by acting in their own self-interest it causes the common resource to be depleted. It contradicts the theory that in a free market, consumers acting in their own self-interest will contribute to overall economic welfare.

Tragedy of the Commons

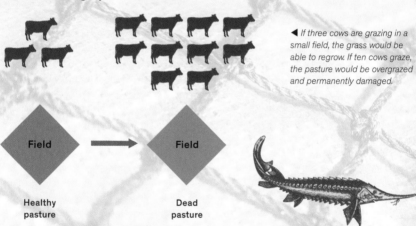

◀ *If three cows are grazing in a small field, the grass would be able to regrow. If ten cows graze, the pasture would be overgrazed and permanently damaged.*

Field → Field

Healthy pasture

Dead pasture

Take, for example, the overgrazing of a shared meadow. If there is only a small number of users, they can graze their cows on the grass and there will be enough time for the grass to regrow. However, if there are too many users, there will be overgrazing and the meadow can be permanently depleted, leaving everyone worse off.

A more modern example is the problem of overfishing. In unregulated seas, modern fishermen were able to catch so much fish that stocks began to dwindle, and in some cases, caused certain fish to become extinct in a particular sea. In the 1970s, mackerel disappeared from the North Sea and cod stocks fell to unsustainable levels.

The problem is that individual fishermen don't have an incentive to limit their catch, even if they know there is a danger of overfishing. If all fishermen reduced their catch by 25 percent, this would allow fish stocks to replenish. But if an individual fisherman reduces his catch, how can he guarantee everyone else will too? There is an incentive for fishermen to free-ride on the moderation of others, on the assumption that, ultimately, fish stocks will inevitably be depleted. Therefore, to protect his own interests, the fisherman might as well maximize his catch now, before there are no more fish to catch. The solution to tragedy of the commons usually relies on government regulation. To prevent overfishing in the North Sea, the European Union put in place a fisheries policy that limited the amount a fisherman could catch. It was controversial because many fishermen saw a decline in revenue or even went out of business. The policy has also struggled to reverse the long-running trend in declining fish stocks that has occurred over the past 50 years. But, Without regulation, fish stocks might have been even further reduced.

PIGOUVIAN TAX

Named after British economist Arthur Pigou (1877–1959), this is a tax based on the principle that "the polluter pays." If consuming or producing a good causes a negative externality, then the consumer or producer should pay a tax on that good. In other words, consumers and producers should pay the full social cost of a good.

Pigou used the example of a good such as alcohol. He argued that the sale of alcohol imposes external costs on society — higher spending on police, prisons and health care. Businesses had a high marginal benefit from selling alcohol, but they didn't face these external costs, which were borne by the police and health care systems.

Cost of beer	+	External cost
$4		Police $1.75 + Health care $2.50

Tax = $4.25

Full cost = $8.25

Suppose that the price of a bottle of beer is $4, and that the external costs to society from alcohol consumption are: $2.50 in higher health care costs associated with damage to liver, and $1.75 in increased crime and social disorder from drunkenness.

This means that the social marginal cost of a bottle of beer is $4 + $2.50 + $1.75 = $8.25.

In a free market, the price of a bottle of beer would be $4. But if these external costs are correct, then the socially efficient price of beer would be $8.25 — more than double the price. The government should place a tax of $4.25 on each bottle.

▲ *The cost of beer is $4, and the external costs are $4.25. A Pigouvian tax would increase beer price by $4.25 to make the final price of beer $8.25 — the full social cost.*

Although demand is likely to be price inelastic (see page 46), the tax may discourage some excess alcohol consumption. The higher price may reduce demand from seven bottles to five on an evening out. And it is these last two bottles which cause the drunkenness that is responsible for most of the external social costs.

TOO MUCH OF A GOOD TAX

If taxes are high, it may encourage people to evade them. A good example is a tax on garbage disposal. There is a logic to taxing garbage — there are external environmental costs to dealing with landfill, and a tax should encourage people to limit the waste they create.

However, if it becomes expensive to dispose of garbage legally, unscrupulous people may resort to illegal fly-tipping. Garbage may be dumped on waste ground and even on city streets — which is an eyesore (itself an external cost) and costs the city even more to deal with. Similarly, if you tax alcohol too much, it may encourage people to brew their own or smuggle alcohol in order to avoid government tax altogether.

▼ *A tax on garbage is good in theory, but can lead to the unintended consequence of discarded items as people avoid the cost of legal disposal.*

SHOULD WE TAX SUGAR?

The World Health Organization
says sugar has many serious health
consequences. It is blamed for the rise in obesity
and health problems such as diabetes and tooth decay.
Consuming sugary drinks therefore imposes an external
cost on society, in particular higher health care costs and
lower economic growth because of ill health. So there
is a good case for a Pigouvian tax on sugary drinks and
food. The money raised could be targeted at improving
health care and education about healthy diet.

▲ Sugar is bad for health and
increases the cost of health care
and dental services for all. A tax
would encourage consumers to
switch to alternative drinks and
raise money to treat the cost of
sugar consumption.

REVENUE NEUTRAL

A higher tax on sugar could be offset by a reduction
in sales tax or income tax. In other words, the
government doesn't increase the overall tax burden,
but only shifts it from one type of goods to the goods
with negative externalities.

Revenue-neutral

◀ If the tax on sugar was increased and raised $10 billion, income tax could be cut by an equivalent $10 billion. The aim of a sugar tax is not to increase overall tax revenue, but to shift taxes onto goods with high social cost.

⬆ Tax on sugar
$10 billion

⬇ Income tax
$10 billion

The point of a Pigouvian tax is not to increase the total tax revenue, but to make consumers and producers pay the full social cost in order to offset the creation of negative externalities. A tax on sugary drinks may be unthinkable, but it could increase social welfare and at the same time encourage the consumption of sugar-free alternatives.

High taxes on tobacco are one reason behind the fall in smoking rates in the Western world since the 1960s. In 1965, 43 percent of adults in the United States smoked. By 2015 only 17.3 percent smoked. By discouraging smoking rates, the tax contributed to rising life expectancy, reduced health costs and increased output from a healthier workforce. The tax has also raised billions of dollars to treat smoking-related diseases. Most people accept tobacco tax as a valid way to raise revenue. Perhaps in the future there will be a similar acceptance of sugar tax.

AGRICULTURE

Across the Western world, agriculture attracts more subsidies than any other industry. In describing conditions of perfect competition, economists often use the examples of many farmers trading apples and pears in a market with many buyers. Yet agriculture is highly susceptible to market failure — which is one reason why it receives the biggest government subsidies.

WHY A GOOD HARVEST MAY BE BAD NEWS FOR FARMERS

Suppose a new chemical fertilizer increases crop yields by 20 percent. Is this good for farmers? At first glance it benefits farmer because they will have increased their output. But if all farmers spend money on the new fertilizer to increase their crop by 20 percent, this can lead to a sharp fall in prices and therefore their income falls.

INELASTIC DEMAND

Demand for agricultural products is relatively inelastic. If supply increases, it can be very hard to sell the extra. People don't tend to eat more carrots just because they are cheaper. If they have excess supply, farmers will cut prices to sell the unwanted food.

A 20 percent increase in supply could cause a sharp drop in prices of 40 percent, but demand may increase

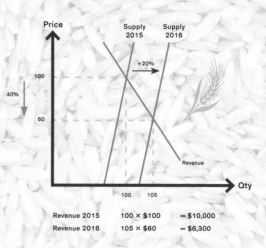

| Revenue 2015 | 100 × $100 | = $10,000 |
| Revenue 2016 | 105 × $60 | = $6,300 |

▲ In 2015, Quantity is 100 and the price $100. In 2016, the quantity supplied rises to 105, causing the price to fall dramatically to $60. This fall in price causes the big drop in revenue for farmers.

by only 5 percent. The increased sales of 5 percent fail to compensate farmers for the fact that carrots have fallen in price by 40 percent. The result is that incomes fall and some farmers go out of business.

So, ironically, this good harvest has caused some farmers to go bankrupt. But if 20 percent of farmers go out of business in one year, the next year, if there is a bad harvest, the result may be a food shortage and higher prices. Agriculture is essentially quite a volatile industry, and there is a case for stabilizing prices and ensuring supply.

COBWEB THEORY

This states that agricultural prices can be volatile.
- Year 1: Shortage of supply. Price rises. High prices encourage more supply for next year.
- Year 2: Supply increases causing prices to fall. Low prices cause farmers to go out of business.
- Year 3: Shortage of supply. Prices rise.

This assumes farmers always base their decisions on last year's prices.

▼ Prices can be volatile in agricultural markets. Oversupply one year can lead to farmers cutting back supply for the next year. However, cutting back supply can cause prices to rise again.

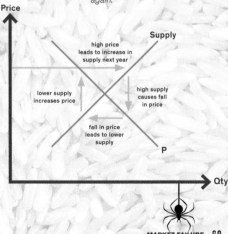

Price

Supply

high price leads to increase in supply next year

lower supply increases price

high supply causes fall in price

fall in price leads to lower supply

P

Qty

GOVERNMENT FAILURE

Government failure occurs when government intervention in the economy creates greater inefficiency and a waste of resources. If we look again at agriculture, there is a justification for government intervention, but in practice governments can end up creating a whole new set of problems.

In the 1970s, the European Union (then called the European Economic Community, or EEC) implemented a Common Agricultural Policy (CAP) to secure prices and supply in its volatile market. They set minimum prices for food and put in place import tariffs to ensure European farmers would receive a guaranteed income.

The problem was that these minimum food prices encouraged farmers to increase supply. They used more chemicals (which damaged the environment) and tried to produce as much as possible — because they were guaranteed to be able to sell at this generous minimum price. It meant higher prices for consumers (who seemed not to notice), and it was also bad news for farmers in other countries who couldn't export to the EEC because of import tariffs.

It was also bad for the European taxpayer. At one point,

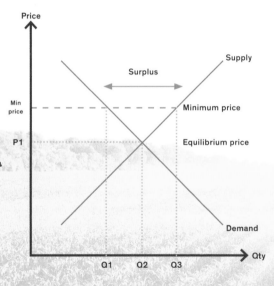

▲ With a minimum price above the equilibrium price of P1, there is a surplus (supply is greater than demand). To maintain price at the minimum, the government needs to buy surplus quantity of Q3-Q1.

the EEC was spending up to 70 percent of its budget on food that nobody wanted to eat. The scheme led to surplus stores of food (the so-called butter mountains and wine lakes). This food was then "dumped" (sold below cost) on world markets, causing farmers in other countries to suffer falling prices and lower incomes (in addition to the high export tariffs to the EEC).

LAW OF UNINTENDED CONSEQUENCES

This states that a regulation to improve one problem may cause an entirely different problem to occur. Agricultural subsidies are intended to stabilize farmers' incomes and ensure the supply of food. But in the EEC, it led to unintended consequences — for the livelihoods of farmers in other countries, excessive use of fertilizers and a growing bill for the taxpayer. Government policy had solved one set of problems (falling prices, shortage of food) but created many new problems as a by-product.

LOBBYING

The next problem governments face is that when a group of business interests get used to generous subsidies, they don't like losing them. Farmers in both Europe and the United States lobby governments very hard to maintain large agricultural subsidies. Taking away subsidies can

make economic sense, but not political sense, and the easiest thing may be to keep paying subsidies to powerful vested interests.

REFORM OF CAP

After many years of hard negotiation, the EU CAP has slowly been reformed, minimum prices have been reduced and the surplus of food has been eradicated. However, farmers still get subsidies — a large proportion linked simply to the amount of land they own (which is very good news for wealthy landowners). It is important to bear in mind that government failure isn't inevitable. It is possible to design subsidies which are linked to environmentally friendly farming and which enhance rural life. It just needs effective planning.

U.S. CORN SYRUP

If you look at the packaging of many food items manufactured in the United States, you will probably see the near-ubiquitous "high-fructose corn syrup." Corn syrup has been linked to obesity, but ironically there is a large subsidy for corn. Between 1995 and 2012, the U.S. spent approximately $277 billion on farm subsidies, of which $81.7 billion subsidized corn production. In effect, the government is subsidizing the junk food industry.

CHAPTER 3

LABOR MARKETS

WAGE DETERMINATION

Why do some elite athletes get paid $200,000 a week for a job many would love to be able to do, but toilet cleaners get paid only $400 a week? Like goods and services, wages are determined by supply- and demand-side factors. The most important factors for determining wages are supply of labor, and economic rent.

SUPPLY OF LABOR

Nearly everyone has the necessary qualifications to be a fruit picker. As long as you are physically capable and willing, it is a job that you could do. Therefore, supply is potentially very high. A small increase in wages would encourage more people to supply their labor for this kind of work.

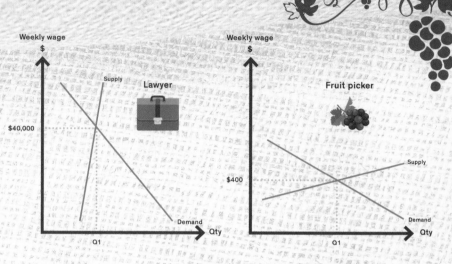

▲ A lawyer gets a much higher wage of $40,000 a week because supply is limited (qualifications are required) and demand is high (firms are willing to pay a high wage). Fruit-picker supply is much greater (many are qualified). The demand is lower (employers are not willing to pay a higher wage) because fruit pickers add less to profits.

But if we take a profession such as law, the number of people qualified to practice is limited. Even if you wanted to become a lawyer, it could take up to five years to get the relevant degree and all the necessary legal training. The supply of labor is inelastic, so even if the salaries of lawyers increased by 10 percent, the number of lawyers wouldn't rise very much.

A good lawyer could save a company millions of dollars in litigation or legal costs. So companies are willing to pay very high fees to get the best lawyers. This combination of a limited supply of lawyers and a willingness to pay high fees means that lawyers can charge very high hourly rates. By contrast, a farmer who grows fruit is unwilling to pay a high wage to fruit pickers because the market is very competitive and costs must be kept down. Demand for labor is wage elastic because many people are willing to do the job. For these reasons, fruit pickers end up with lower wages than lawyers.

ECONOMIC RENT

This is the difference between the wage you are willing to do the job for and the wage you actually receive. For fruit-pickers, the economic rent may be very low. The wage they receive is likely to be just above the minimum rate for which they would be willing to work. But for a top soccer player, the economic rent may be very high. Lionel Messi may be willing to play soccer for €1,000 a week. But the supply of players with the skills of Lionel Messi is one — supply is perfectly inelastic. And if Messi plays well and scores 50 goals per season, this is worth millions of euros for his football club in terms of revenue. And that's why Lionel Messi enjoys a very high economic rent.

▶ *"There's only one Lionel Messi." This is very helpful for negotiating a wage contract. Messi can use his scarcity and profitability to demand a very high wage.*

DIVISION OF LABOR

Division of labor occurs when workers are given specific tasks within the production process. If you ask a worker to make a car, how long would it take? Weeks, months, perhaps even years. But if you ask a worker to fit car wheels on an assembly line, he or she may be able to work on a thousand or more cars in a day.

A complex manufacturing process like building a car naturally lends itself to division of labor. The advantages of division of labor are:

- Workers need less training, and even unskilled workers can become very productive.
- It can improve health and safety because workers don't have to move around the factory and fewer tools are needed.

- Workers can concentrate on what they are best at.
- An increase in productivity can mean higher wages for workers.

> Of necessity, he who pursues a very specialized task will do it best.
> Xenophon, Greek philosopher
> *Cyropaedia*, 370 BCE

Division of labor

ASSEMBLY LINE

◀ *A single worker would struggle to build a car, if ever. Many specialized workers can make mass production a possibility.*

One worker   Many workers

DIVISION OF LABOR AND HENRY FORD

• •

The American industrialist Henry Ford wasn't the first person to use an assembly line, but in 1913 he used division of labor and assembly lines on a scale not seen before. His new automobile production systems were so efficient that the price of a Ford Model T car fell 30 percent between 1908 and 1912. He was able to pay workers five times the average wage and reduce the average hourly week. Cars could be produced so quickly that he had to use Japanese black paint because it was the only paint to dry quickly enough. The revolution in assembly lines was soon copied all around the world, causing the price of manufactured goods to fall and workers' real wages to increase.

PROBLEMS WITH DIVISION OF LABOR

Working on an assembly line can become very boring and repetitive, even with a generous salary. The result may be high labor turnover — in other words, some new workers won't stay in the job very long!

Karl Marx criticized division of labor for causing the alienation of workers. In the 19th century, American philosophers like Ralph Waldo Emerson and Henry David Thoreau (1817–62) were already worried that division of labor caused citizens to become detached from the process of production. Perhaps because mass-produced products lack the personal touch, there has been a resurgence of interest in handmade goods as Western societies have become better off, although these niche products are only a small part of the market.

MINIMUM WAGES

Minimum wages are a government regulation that prevents companies from paying less than a certain hourly rate. The aim of minimum wages is to increase the income of the low-paid and reduce inequality. However, critics argue that if the rate is set too high, it can lead to unemployment.

BENEFITS WITH A MINIMUM WAGE

- Higher pay for the lowest earners. Inequality has increased in recent years, and a minimum wage helps reduce the wage gap.
- Higher wages can act as an incentive for companies to improve labor productivity by, for example, investing in technology that makes labor more effective. In the long term, a high-wage, high-skilled labor force is usually better for the economy than trying to maintain competitiveness through low pay.
- Increased labor market participation. People such as students, the unemployed and parents with children have more incentive to enter a labor market with higher wages.
- With a decline in trade unions, many workers have a limited ability to bargain for higher wages.

PROBLEMS WITH MINIMUM WAGE

The biggest problem with increasing the minimum wage is that it leads to higher costs for companies and may cause them to take on fewer workers. In theory, a minimum wage can cause unemployment.

With minimum wages above the equilibrium, demand falls and supply increases, creating the unemployed labor of Q3-Q2. A minimum wage may also encourage people to avoid labor-market regulations. This could involve working in the "hidden economy" or it could involve workers reclassifying themselves as self-employed. This could even lead to workers being more exploited than before.

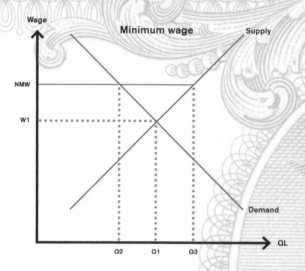

▲ Initially, supply of workers = demand for workers giving a wage of W1. If the government imposes a national minimum wage (NMW), the supply of workers is greater than the demand — leading to unemployment in the amount Q3–Q2.

EMPIRICAL EVIDENCE

There have been numerous studies into the effects that increasing the minimum wage has on employment. The majority have found that increasing the minimum wage — at relatively low levels — has led to little unemployment. It appears that where the demand for labor is inelastic, companies are willing to pay workers a higher wage. But labor markets are not perfectly competitive, and sometimes companies have monopsonic power (monopoly power in setting wages, see page 110). So some companies are able to set artificially low wages and the minimum wage helps to correct this.

WINNERS AND LOSERS

The impact of a minimum wage is not uniform. Some sectors will be more affected. Hair salons, for example, are very dependent on wage costs, as a rise in the minimum wage will cause a significant increase in labor costs, which could make them unprofitable. Profitable multinationals can absorb wage increases, but small independent retailers running at break-even may be adversely affected.

MONOPSONY

Monopsony is a situation in which a company has market power in employing workers. A pure monopsony is when workers have only one potential employer. In this situation, the workers are effectively wage takers. If they don't accept a low-paid job, they will have no work at all.

Examples of monopsony may include:
- Firemen employed by government.
- Workers in a town with one major employer, e.g., coal mine, cotton mill.

Monopsonies were common during the Industrial Revolution, when one big employer often dominated a town or village. In those days, uneducated workers without transport had a limited ability to move around and seek different kinds of work. They were often captive workers vulnerable to exploitation by the area's major employer.

◀ The Industrial Revolution created large powerful firms that often dominated whole towns. Choice of employment was often limited to the local factory or mine.

$100

$80

Trade Union

Monopsony

◀ *A powerful monopsony can cut wages to $80, but if workers form a trade union they can try to bargain for wages to rise back up to $100.*

The theory of monopsony suggests that companies can maximize profits by employing fewer workers at lower wages than in a competitive market. It is socially inefficient, because there is less output, fewer workers are employed and workers receive lower wages. The only winner is the company, which enjoys higher profits.

TRADES UNIONS VS. MONOPSONY

In the late 19th century, many workers felt wages were too low and working conditions unfair. In response to the power of monopsonistic employers, workers started to form trade unions.

The aim of trade unions was to increase wages for workers and provide better working conditions.

Trade unions could counter-balance the power of employers by threatening to go on strike. Strike action could cause loss of profits for firms. Sometimes firms did respond to trade unions by increasing wages and improving working conditions, but not often. Firms had more resources (profit) to ride out strikes, forcing workers back into work for the same wages.

IS THERE MONOPSONY TODAY?

In theory, workers have the ability to find a job that pays higher wages. But in practice it can be difficult for workers to move jobs. It can require a lot of time, preparation and interviews to get a new job. Many workers will stay with their existing employer rather than seek out a job with only marginally higher wages. There is also significant geographical immobility — it is hard to move to London or New York, where jobs are more available, but the cost of living is high.

LUMP OF LABOR FALLACY

The lump of labor fallacy relates to the contention that the amount of work available in an economy is fixed. If there are a fixed number of jobs available, then it could be argued that immigrants take jobs or potential jobs from workers already in the employment market.

However, the idea there is a fixed number of jobs is claimed to be a fallacy. Immigrants who find work earn income to spend in the rest of the economy, creating new jobs — so the number of jobs is not fixed. Immigration increases labor supply, but also increases demand for labor. And immigrants may take so-called 3D jobs — so-called because they are dirty, dangerous and demeaning — that companies would otherwise find difficult to fill.

If a country experiences net migration, these new workers will spend their wages on goods and services,

▼ *Immigration increases the size of the population, but also increases the number of jobs available.*

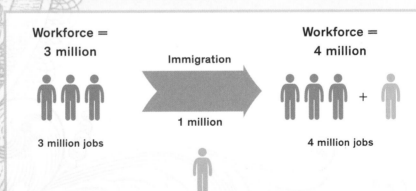

Workforce = 3 million

Immigration 1 million

Workforce = 4 million

3 million jobs

4 million jobs

MASS IMMIGRATION IN THE U.S.

• • • • • • • • • • • • •

Between 1880 and 1920, the U.S. absorbed more than 20 million immigrants. This did not cause a rise in unemployment, but helped the U.S. economy to rapidly expand, making it the largest in the world. During this period, the real wages of workers rose.

which creates additional demand and therefore additional jobs. There will be a rise in aggregate demand and companies will need to take on more workers to satisfy the growing economy. In other words, immigrants tend to create as many new jobs as they fill. If the population expands, the number of available jobs does not stay constant, but increases.

IMMIGRATION IN A TIME OF UNEMPLOYMENT?

If an economy has high unemployment and net inward migration, do immigrants cause more unemployment in this case? The principle is the same. Immigrants may get jobs, but this doesn't necessarily increase the overall unemployment rate. All things being equal, the new labor supply will increase the demand for labor. The problem is that those who are unemployed may feel that they have missed out on jobs that go to immigrants. But immigration itself is not the cause of unemployment. The cause of unemployment could be due to cyclical factors (such as recession) or structural factors (such as a lack of relevant skills).

CRITICISM OF THE LUMP OF LABOR FALLACY

Some argue the lump of labor fallacy may not always be true, and in some circumstances immigration may cause job losses.

Firstly, if migrants come to the United States and are willing to accept low wages, existing job-seekers may experience real-wage unemployment — they don't find work because they are not willing to work for significantly lower wages.

And what if immigrants find jobs but send the majority of their wages back to their countries of origin? In this case, the increase in domestic aggregate demand would be limited. However, in practice, immigrants need to spend a relatively high percentage of their wages to cover the cost of living.

And of course some immigrants have significantly higher skill levels than native workers. In this case, employers needing to fill skilled job vacancies are likely to prefer high-skilled migrants over low-skilled native workers.

DOES CUTTING THE AVERAGE WORKING WEEK INCREASE EMPLOYMENT?

Some argue that in order to reduce unemployment, the government should cut the number of hours that can be worked. Suppose workers are currently working 40 hours per week, and the government imposes a maximum working week of 30 hours. The argument is that companies would need to employ more workers to make up for the shortfall. Individual workers may have lower incomes (because they work fewer hours) but society benefits because more jobs are created.

This sounds logical, but cutting the number of hours worked per week may not in practice solve unemployment. There are costs involved in employing more workers — administration costs, costs of training and increased management costs. So companies may respond by trying to increase productivity without increasing the size of the workforce. If workers have their hours cut and wages fall, then they are likely reduce their spending, leading to lower demand.

Cutting hours

(1) 10 people x 40 hours → 400 hours

(2) 11.4 people x 35 hours → 400 hours

Cutting hours to 35 means firms need to employ 1.4 more people

◄ This argument states that cutting the working week from 40 to 35 hours creates more jobs and therefore reduces unemployment.

Moreover, companies may not be able to employ sufficiently skilled labor. The skills and experience of many managers and workers are indispensable — you can't necessarily replicate those skills and experience when you hire someone new. Labor is much more variable than other factors of production.

FRANCE'S 35-HOUR WORKING WEEK

• • • • • • •

In Febraury 2000, in France, the government implemented a maximum working week of 35 hours. It is relatively popular with workers, who have a short working week. But there is little evidence that it has reduced unemployment. In the period 2010–16, unemployment in France has been significantly higher than in countries such as the U.S. and the UK, which have more flexible labor markets. One argument is that labor-market restrictions, such as the 35-hour working week, actively discourage firms from employing workers in the first place.

GENDER INEQUALITY

In most Western economies, the average pay of women is less than that of men. The pay gap has narrowed in recent decades, but often women are paid 20 percent less than men. Which economic theories can explain this?

Qualifications. In the past, men were more likely to get degrees and professional qualifications, which could explain higher pay. However, in recent years this education gap has narrowed, and even comparing equal education standards, we still see a pay gap. Ten years after graduation, women with advanced degrees still earn only 77 percent as much as men with the same qualifications.

Productivity of labor. In heavy manual labor, men had an advantage. But with modern economies becoming essentially service sector-based, this is no longer applicable. In the modern economy, the demand for labor comes from knowledge and service-sector skills rather than from shifting lumps of coal.

Market forces. One area where there is an obvious pay gap is in sports. In most sports, men get paid a lot more than their female counterparts. In some sports, like tennis, the gap has narrowed significantly. But in sports like soccer and hockey, there is significantly more money in the men's game than the women's. To alter the wage structure you would need to see a huge growth in women's baseball and more demand for female baseball players.

Discrimination. In the not-too-distant past, you could have a factory in which women were paid less than men for doing effectively the same task. This was blatant discrimination, which was outlawed in the United States by the Equal Pay Act of 1963. Since the Act was passed, women's earnings have risen from 60 percent of men's earnings in 1960 to 80 percent in 2016.

Glass ceiling. It is easy to legislate against paying different groups of workers a different wage for doing exactly the same job. But it is more difficult to discriminate against employers who may not be as likely to promote women or people from ethnic minorities. If you get a lower hourly wage, it is fairly straightforward; but if you don't get promoted, how can we know whether it is because of discrimination or other factors? Some have suggested that the limited number of women in top posts and boardrooms is due to an invisible glass ceiling — a metaphor for the reluctance to hire women for the highest-paying jobs.

Overtime. One reason that is suggested for the higher earnings of men is that they dominate blue-collar jobs that require extra payment for overtime. White-collar service sector jobs are less likely to receive overtime payments.

Career breaks. Perhaps the strongest explanation for the continued wage differential is the impact on career earnings when women take breaks to have children. At the age of 35, women's pay is 90 percent of men's, but in the age group 55–64 it has fallen to 74 percent of men's. Taking a break to have children means women lose skills needed in the workplace and are therefore less likely to be promoted and progress up the pay scale. Another factor is that a company has an incentive to hire a worker who isn't going to take maternity leave, which may require the company to cover maternity pay and find a replacement worker. You could say this leads to discrimination against women because companies want to avoid the costs of maternity leave. From the company's perspective, it is an effort to minimize costs.

ECONOMICS OF AN AGING POPULATION

It is well known that Western society has an aging population. The U.S. census of 2014 estimates that between 2012 and 2050 the number of people aged 65 and over will increase from 43.1 million to 83.7 million, nearly doubling the number of senior citizens.

The old-age dependency ratio in the U.S. (which is calculated by dividing the population aged 65 and over by the population aged 18–64 and multiplying by 100):

- 1940 — 11 percent.
- 2010 — 21 percent.
- 2050 — 36 percent.

The rise in the old-age dependency ratio is a challenge for the U.S., but it is an even bigger challenge for countries like Italy and Japan. Japan is forecast to see a rise from 30 percent in 2005 to a problematic 70 percent in 2050.

The rise in the proportion of senior citizens is due to the baby-boomer generation of the 1960s reaching old age and a significant rise in life expectancy.

THE IMPACT OF AN AGING POPULATION

- **Tax revenues.** People who have retired pay less income tax and make lower social security contributions. It is also hard to raise taxes on those who are not working.

- **Rise in entitlement spending.** This refers to spending commitments promised by governments. It includes health care and social-security pensions.

- **Budget deficit.** The combination of falling tax revenues and higher government spending gives governments exactly the kind of dilemma they don't want. Meeting the needs of an aging population may require higher rates of taxation — without any obvious benefit to workers hit by higher taxes — just to meet the growing health care and pensions bill.

- **Shortage of workers.** With an aging population, the working population becomes a smaller share of the population. Will the economy be able to fill vacancies, especially in areas like health care?

- **Changing sectors within the economy.** An ageing population will see a shift in sectors — perhaps a decline in education and rise in the importance of health care.

- **Saving.** An aging population will also have different spending and saving habits. A relatively higher level of saving could cause greater demand for government bonds to provide income in retirement.

IS IT ALL DOOM AND GLOOM?

It is easy to get carried away with doomsday scenarios — that an ageing population means an inevitable and unsustainable rise in government borrowing. We should remember that the United States and other major economies have already coped with previous rises in the old-age dependency ratio. The percentage of seniors doubled between 1940 and 2010 — yet in that time living standards have increased significantly. The economy has absorbed the growth in the dependency ratio without any obvious ill effects thanks to economic growth and improved technology. If economic growth continues, there will be a bigger national income with which to pay for increased health care costs.

SOLUTIONS TO AN AGING POPULATION

• •

- **Raise retirement age.** One obvious solution to an aging population is to raise the retirement age, based on average life expectancy and the percentage of seniors in the population as a whole. If people live longer, we need to raise retirement age to maintain this percentage.

- **Semi-retirement.** The modern service-sector economy means that divisions between working and retirement are less clear cut. There are more opportunities for people to continue working, at least part-time, past retirement age.

- **Immigration.** Immigration is a hotly contested political issue, but it remains an excellent solution to a rapidly aging population. Migrants tend to be of working age and so help to limit the growth in the old-age dependency ratio. Japan has very strict laws on immigration and has suffered one of the sharpest rises in the old-age dependency ratio. Without immigration, it has also struggled to fill unpopular manual jobs like construction.

IS IT FAIR TO RAISE THE RETIREMENT AGE?

If people live longer, there is logic behind raising the retirement age. A higher retirement age has the benefit of reducing government spending on pensions, increasing tax revenue and increasing the productive capacity of the economy. No wonder it is popular with economists, but there is an issue of equality — raising the retirement age will affect some workers more than others.

High-income earners have the disposable income to invest in a private pension or retirement savings and pay off their mortgage. Therefore, the increase in retirement age doesn't really matter to them — they can retire on their personal funds anyway. Low-income earners paying a high percentage of income on rent do not have this luxury and will have to continue working.

In addition, many low-income jobs are more physically demanding. If you work full-time in a warehouse lifting boxes, until you are 70 years old, retirement may be very challenging. Many economists and politicians arguing for a higher retirement age probably have a comfortable desk job or private savings they can use for early retirement.

Finally, when people started their working life, they may have assumed that the retirement age would remain at 65 and budgeted accordingly. If the retirement age is increased to 70 years old they may feel cheated.

INCOME AND SUBSTITUTION EFFECT

If your hourly wage increased from $10 an hour to $20 an hour, would you work more, or less? Most people would work more, because the wage is now more attractive. If your hourly wage increased from $10 an hour to $10,000 an hour, would you work more or less? Most people would work less, because you can get your target income by working fewer hours.

Supply of labor

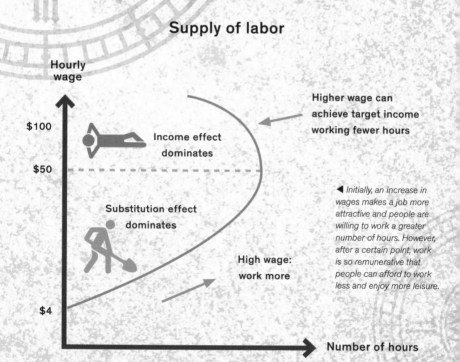

Hourly wage

Higher wage can achieve target income working fewer hours

$100

Income effect dominates

$50

Substitution effect dominates

High wage: work more

$4

Number of hours

◄ *Initially, an increase in wages makes a job more attractive and people are willing to work a greater number of hours. However, after a certain point, work is so remunerative that people can afford to work less and enjoy more leisure.*

You might not realize it, but in answering these questions you are wrestling with the income and substitution effects. The substitution effect states that with a higher wage, work is relatively more attractive than leisure (in other words, not working). In simple terms, a higher wage gives you a greater incentive to work more.

However, the income effect states that with a higher wage, you can reach your target income by working fewer hours, and you can afford more leisure time. If you are paid $10,000 an hour, you could work one eight-hour day a year and earn $80,000. For some people that would be all the income they need — they could spend the rest of the year travelling around the world. If you earn $10,000 an hour, you are unlikely to feel the need to work a 45-hour week to meet the bills.

For some people, the substitution effect will be more powerful than the income effect. A higher wage encourages you to work more, but for those with limited needs, the income effect may dominate. Bear in mind that each individual is different.

A student working in a fast-food restaurant needs to earn $15,000 a year to fund their college education. They don't really enjoy selling burgers — and would rather be studying for exams. If there is a rise in hourly wages, they can work fewer hours to achieve their target income. It helps that working in a restaurant is often flexible, and they can probably ask to reduce their hours.

Another individual may have more expenses than the student, and they happen to derive satisfaction from driving an expensive car and wearing designer clothes. If their hourly wage rises, they are happy because they can earn more money and buy more luxury goods. In this case, the substitution effect dominates, and they are now willing to do some overtime.

WORK–LIFE BALANCE

In the past, many economists predicted that rising real wages would cause people to work shorter hours.

In the first part of the 20th century this did occur, with both rising real wages and a fall in the average working week from 60 to 40 hours. In other words, if real wages rise, you can have a higher income *and* work less.

In 1930, John Maynard Keynes wrote an essay titled "Economic Possibilities for Our Grandchildren," which suggested that in the future people would work a 15-hour week.

So far, this prediction has failed to materialize. In 2014, the average full-time American worker worked 47 hours a week.

Keynes predicted a 15-hour week and rising wages. But in the post-war period this shortening of the average working week has halted, and in recent decades we have seen people work longer hours. Why would people work longer hours despite an increase in real wages?

- A perception of rising living costs.
- They may enjoy work or at least find it difficult to cut hours. American economist Richard Freeman

stated that in the second half of the 20th century in the U.S., "the workaholic rich replaced the idle rich."

- According to U.S. President Theodore Roosevelt, "Far and away the best prize that life has to offer is the chance to work hard at work worth doing." In other words, for many people the goal of life is not to maximize leisure opportunities but to work hard at a worthwhile job.
- Firms don't want their trained employees to work fewer hours. Even if you want to work fewer hours, you may not be given the option.
- There are always more goods to buy. Fifty years ago, there weren't as many designer clothes, foreign holidays and electronic gadgets, which are now perceived as more essential.

FEWER HOURS

• • • • • •

For the self-employed working at home, the internet has made it possible to earn a good income while working fewer hours. The popularity of Timothy Ferriss' 2007 book *The 4-Hour Workweek* suggests that at least some people are aspiring to work less. Although, it is rare to find someone who manages to actually work just four hours a week.

CHAPTER 4

BUSINESS ECONOMICS

EFFICIENCY

Efficiency is concerned with the optimal production and distribution of resources.

There are different types of efficiency:

- Productive efficiency — producing goods for the lowest average cost.
- Allocative efficiency — optimal distribution of goods, making sure the benefit to consumers is equivalent to the cost of production.
- Dynamic efficiency — improving efficiency over time. In 1928, the Ford Motor Company was the most efficient car producer, but by the 1970s it had slipped behind Japanese competitors, having failed to increase productivity at the same rate.
- Social efficiency — including all the externalities as well as private cost and benefits.

WHY ARE THERE DIFFERENT TYPES OF EFFICIENCY?

In communist economies, government five-year plans often led to huge increases in the output of steel, army boots, wheat, and so on. To achieve these ambitious targets, great effort and efficiencies were made; the problem was that people did not necessarily need or want all that steel, all those army boots and so much wheat.

In other words, there was productive efficiency (producing for low cost), but not allocative efficiency (distributing according to needs and preferences). There was a story of a Soviet boot factory that made thousands of pairs of boots, but because supply was greater than

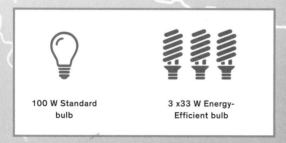

100 W Standard bulb

3 x33 W Energy-Efficient bulb

◀ 100 watts of energy illuminates one standard light bulb, however 100 watts of energy illuminates three new energy-efficient light bulbs, giving more light for the same energy.

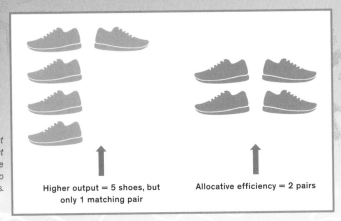

▶ *Higher output creates five shoes, but only one pair. Allocative efficiency creates two pairs of shoes.*

Higher output = 5 shoes, but only 1 matching pair

Allocative efficiency = 2 pairs

demand, they would burn the surplus every week. But the factory was rewarded for exceeding its output quotas. Producing efficiently uses the fewest resources per unit of output, but it isn't the only factor to consider.

EFFICIENCY AND EQUITY

Another issue is the potential trade-off between efficiency and equity. If a state-owned monopoly is privatized, the new owners will seek to increase profits and cut costs. To be more efficient they can make surplus workers redundant. This makes the economy more efficient, but can have a negative impact on unemployment and equity (at least in the short term).

Similarly, zero-hour labor contracts may increase efficiency for a company.

If business is slow, a company can pay workers for just the five hours they are needed for. If demand is high, it can pay workers for 40 hours. This reduces the company's costs and increases efficiency — but for the worker it will mean there are some weeks when their pay is very low. The pursuit of efficiency goals can encourage firms to push workers to their limits, but this can be counterproductive if the workers become demotivated or take too many risks — for example, delivery drivers who are paid per item.

EFFICIENCY WAGE THEORY

This theory states that increasing wages may be more efficient, because workers who are paid higher wages are more loyal, motivated and productive.

ECONOMIES OF SCALE

Among the most important types of efficiency are economies of scale. These occur when higher output reduces long-run average costs.

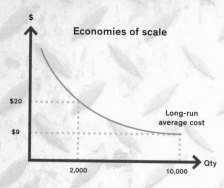

▲ Producing 2,000 units gives an average cost of $20. Increasing output to 10,000 units reduces average costs to $9.

If a large car factory produced one car, the average cost of a car would be very high. As more cars are produced, the average cost falls. If you have a big outlay to set up a factory, you need to produce a lot to make it efficient.

WHAT CAUSES ECONOMIES OF SCALE?

Spreading of fixed costs. If it costs $100 million to build a factory, and it produces just one car, the average fixed cost would be $100m. If it produces 500,000, the average fixed cost of the factory is $200.

Specialization. The production of a motor car or computer is now so specialized that production usually takes place across the globe. Raw materials for batteries may come from Africa; the good is designed in the U.S.; the components are then assembled in Asia. This is more efficient, but requires a very high scale of output.

Division of labor. Splitting up the production process into different tasks enables workers to be more specialized. But if you have thousands of different jobs on an assembly line, you need a high output to make it worthwhile.

Transport economies. If you transport one can of paint, the average transport cost may be $5. If you transport 1 million cans of paint, the average transport cost per can would be very low, perhaps $0.01.

Container principle. One of the most significant causes of improved trade and living standards in post-war periods came from something very ordinary and unexciting — the shipping container. This was more efficient because:

- It saved labor. Previously, each box was lifted and stacked by dock workers in shipyards. Containers could hold hundreds of boxes and be lifted by a crane.
- It was more efficient to export higher quantities of goods.
- It prevented pilfering. Dock workers might be tempted to pocket a few of their favorite items while unloading.

Modern trade theory. One aspect of modern trade theory is that it doesn't matter what a country specializes in, as long as it specializes in something. Economies of scale are so important that they may outweigh any other comparative advantage.

Diseconomies of scale is when higher output leads to higher long-run average costs. The problem with the division of labor is that the job can become very boring, and workers may become demotivated. If you spend all day putting tires on car wheels, you will get bored and may start to shirk your job. Furthermore, some companies have found that increasing the size of the workforce can be counterproductive — it is harder to motivate workers in a very big workforce. If you work in a small team of 10, your effort (or lack of effort) will be more noticeable. If you are a relatively anonymous worker in a team of 200, it is easier to do little work.

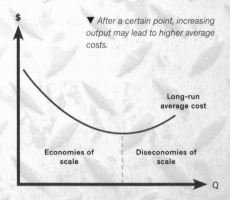

▼ *After a certain point, increasing output may lead to higher average costs.*

PRICE DISCRIMINATION

Price discrimination involves charging a different price to different groups of consumers for the same good.

If you ever buy an airplane or train ticket, you will see numerous examples of price discrimination:

- Discounts for age groups.
- Discounts for buying in advance.
- Different prices at different times of the year.
- Different prices at different times of the day.

HOW DOES PRICE DISCRIMINATION OCCUR?

We know that some consumers are willing to pay higher prices, some are not — there are different elasticities of demand (see page 46). For a businessman who needs to go to a meeting, his demand is likely to be inelastic — he can't travel at another time, and he can expense the ticket. But a student who has more flexibility, lower income and less need to travel will be more price sensitive — her demand is elastic. So business travelers who book at the last minute will pay much higher prices. For a student willing to book in advance, prices are lower.

The train company is trying to maximize profits by increasing price in time segments with inelastic demand (peak time), and cutting prices in time segments with elastic demand (off-peak).

A ticket priced at $70 would not sell very well at off-peak times, and reducing the price to $50 may increase demand significantly. At peak times, increasing the price from $50 to $70 may cause only a small fall in demand.

To be successful, a company needs market power (the ability to set prices)

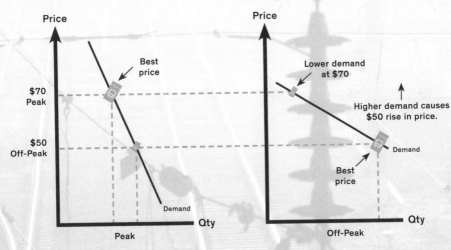

▲ *At peak times, the firm maximizes profits by charging $70. However, this price would be inappropriate for off-peak because demand would be very low. For off-peak, a reduction in price to $50 leads to increased demand and increased revenue.*

and also the ability to separate markets. This is why train companies give discounts by age — a student discount during off-peak times is not an act of charity toward hard-up students, but an attempt to increase revenue from students with price-elastic demand.

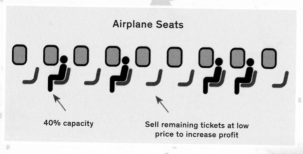

Airplane Seats

40% capacity

Sell remaining tickets at low price to increase profit

◄ When a plane is scheduled to fly, empty seats are wasted revenue. Even if the remaining seats were sold at a low price, the firm would increase revenue and thus profits because extra passengers add very little to overall costs.

FILLING AN AIRPLANE

The reason why there are so many different ticket prices for flights is due to another factor. An airline has an incentive to fill its planes. The costs of a full plane at 100 percent capacity aren't much more than those of a plane at 20 percent capacity — there is a low marginal cost of extra passengers.

If a plane has many empty seats, a company can increase revenue by selling the remaining tickets at a low price — some revenue is better than none. But if a flight is proving very popular, the airline company can raise prices to make sure that only those willing to pay high prices get the remaining tickets.

NO USE CRYING OVER SPILLED MILK

Using price discrimination to fill up an airplane is similar to the principle of "no use crying over spilled milk." Suppose you buy 50 Christmas trees for $5, and sell 30 for $10. On Christmas Eve you are left with 20 trees. If you keep the price at $10, you may sell only a few. It is better to sell below cost to maximize revenue. In other words, it is better to get $2 per surplus tree than $0 when they don't sell at $10. Selling the remaining trees at $2 also saves the cost of disposing of them.

Once you have bought 50 trees, that cost is lost. It is a sunk cost, and you can't get it back. Similarly, once an airline timetables a flight, most costs are sunk — the airline may as well sell as many tickets as it can. This is why it can be rational for companies to sell some goods below cost as a way of maximizing revenue and thereby minimizing losses.

WHY YOU SHOULD BOOK FIRST

Suppose you and 49 friends decide to go on a group vacation on the same flight. You should try to book your seat right away. If you wait for your friends to book the flight, it will probably be more expensive! This is because, as the airplane gets close to filling up, the airline will increase prices for last few tickets, in the hope that those with inelastic demand will buy them.

BARRIERS TO ENTRY

Barriers to entry are factors that make it difficult for new companies to enter an industry. Why are some industries dominated by one or two companies, while other industries are very competitive?

There are many companies that would like a slice of Google's profits, but competing with them is not so straightforward. By comparison, it is relatively easy to set yourself up as a tour guide in a major city. Barriers of entry can be complex and varied:

Barriers to Entry

1. Size: the established firm has large size economies of scale.
2. Brand recognition: the established firm has brand recognition, whereas the new firm has none.
3. Retail: stores want to stock established brands and not take risk with a new firm.

Small Entrant   vs.   Established Firm

Stores don't want to stock new, untried products

Small size, no economies of scale

Small entrant = no brand recognition

Stores prefer to stock existing brand familiar to market

Large size, economies of scale

Established firm = brand recognition

◀ *In many industries, new entrants are at a disadvantage. New small firms struggle to compete against existing firms because they lack economies of scale and brand recognition.*

makes it very difficult for new entrants to capture any share of the market. Apart from Pepsi, very few companies could compete with the advertising budget of Coca-Cola.

Multiple brands. Some companies are clever at creating monopoly power. It may seem that the market for laundry detergent offers numerous choices, but if you look behind the brands, you will notice they are owned by a small number of companies with monopoly power. Multiple brands give the illusion of competition and make it harder for new companies to enter the market — they would be competing for one-thirtieth of the market share rather than half.

Sometimes, monopolies can arise almost by accident. Facebook was the first company to create a global social media platform which took off. It is now difficult to compete that Facebook because there is an incentive for any new users to join the network thatmost people are already on. Facebook retains monopoly power because it was the first and most extensive such platform to gain wide traction.

Minimum efficient scale. If a carmaker only reaches the lowest point on its long-run average costs at 400,000 cars, this makes it very difficult for a new carmaker to enter the market. Even if it sells 100,000, it will be relatively inefficient and unable to compete.

Brand loyalty. Why has Apple amassed $250 billion of retained profit over the past few years? They have tremendous brand loyalty from consumers who are willing to keep buying new Apple products. We know they are expensive, but we keep buying.

Advertising. Advertising can play a major role in creating this brand loyalty. Coca-Cola has a marketing budget of $3.5 billion per year, which enables it to constantly reinforce its dominant brand image. The ubiquity of Coca-Cola

MONOPOLY

A pure monopoly occurs when there is one company operating in an industry, though a company is considered to have monopoly power when it controls significant market share. For example, Google has up to 80 percent of the search-engine market.

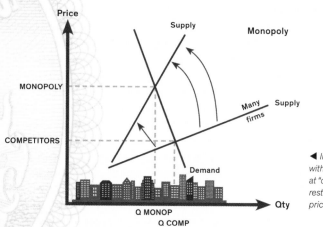

◀ In a competitive market with many firms, the price is at "competitors." A monopoly restricts supply and increases price to "monopoly."

ARE MONOPOLIES BAD FOR CONSUMERS?

Monopolies are usually considered harmful for consumers because they increase prices and reduce efficiency.

High prices. In 1999, a U.S. federal judge investigating abuse of monopoly power by Microsoft found that it charged a revenue-maximizing price of $89 for Windows 98,

much higher than a competitive price of $49, which would still have been profitable.

Inefficiency. It is argued that if a company has monopoly power, it has an "easy life" — it can be profitable without making much effort, so there is less incentive to innovate, cut costs and offer a better service. It is said to have been one of the failings of state-owned companies in Eastern Europe — a lack of competition encouraged inefficiency.

Less choice. For example, in the early days of TV, there was no option but to watch the one or two channels that were available. Satellite TV has enabled a huge range of choices, covering almost every niche imaginable.

CAN MONOPOLIES BE GOOD FOR CONSUMERS?

Economists argue that monopolies can in certain circumstances be beneficial.

Profit for research and development. If the pharmaceutical market was perfectly competitive, companies would make low profits and lack the capacity to invest in developing new treatments. High profits and the promise of temporary monopoly power give large pharmaceutical companies the capacity and incentive to undertake long and difficult trials that may ultimately benefit consumers with better medicines. Standard Oil, though widely reviled as a powerful monopoly, did help to develop more products from oil.

Natural monopolies. Some industries cannot be broken up into small companies because the economies of scale are so high that it would be inefficient. An alternative is for monopolies to be regulated by governments, by, for example, setting price limits on tap water and electricity.

Monopolies are successful. It is argued that monopoly can lead to inefficiency. Another way of looking at this is to say that companies gain monopoly power because they have a unique selling point.

Apple has monopoly power thanks to strong brand loyalty, but this is because it offers attractive products. And it is not true that monopolies necessarily become lazy. For example, Google is still innovative, allowing workers the ability to develop new products. Here, the monopoly power of Google enables more innovation because the company can afford to take risks and employ a highly skilled workforce.

STANDARD OIL — THE TEXTBOOK MONOPOLY

In the late 19th century, John D. Rockefeller founded Standard Oil, a company that came to symbolize the "Gilded Age" — and the excesses of monopoly power. By 1890, Standard Oil controlled 88 percent of the highly lucrative business of refined oil flows in the United States.

At first, Standard Oil grew organically, but then it sought to buy its rivals, closing down any inefficient companies. Enjoying high profits, Standard could afford to undercut rivals by selling below the cost of production, causing rival companies to go out of business. Once it had monopoly power, it could increase prices again. And by colluding with railroad companies, it was able to transport oil much more cheaply than its rivals (see Collusion, page 114).

In 1911, the U.S. Supreme Court found Standard Oil in violation of the 1890 Sherman antitrust laws. The company was split up into 34 smaller companies (including companies that became Exxon, Amoco, Mobil and Chevron). However, the founder, John D. Rockefeller, had the last laugh when the shares of the 34 new companies doubled in value — making him even richer than before.

MODERN MONOPOLIES

• • • • • • • • • • • •

In the modern age, Microsoft would often be able to preload both Microsoft Windows and Internet Explorer on a new computer. For a long time, this gave Microsoft monopoly power in both internet browsers (Internet Explorer) and office products (Windows and Microsoft Office).

COLLUSION

Collusion occurs when companies work together to set higher prices and maximize profits in an industry. Collusion is usually illegal because it means higher prices for consumers, with little by way of compensation. Despite severe penalties for collusion, the temptation to make higher profits can be hard to resist.

Suppose we have a competitive market, with two gas stations charging $2 per gallon. This low price enables each to make an annual profit of $1 million. However, if they agree to set a profit-maximizing price of $4 per gallon, they could make supernormal profits of $4 million each.

▼ *Low prices and a competitive market = low profit. Collusion, where both increase prices, enables both to make high profit.*

Game Theory

High price	Firm A = $4m	Firm B = $4m	Collusion
Low price	Firm A = $1m	Firm B = $1m	Competition

At $4 per gallon they would sell slightly less gas, but because demand is inelastic and people will continue to fill up their cars, revenue would increase.

INCENTIVE TO COLLUDE
Suppose several companies agree to increase the price to $4 per gallon — they sell less, but overall profits increase. However, one company may decide to make even more

profit by undercutting the other firms. By selling at $2.50 per gallon it benefits both from the high price in the industry and from the high output, generating even bigger profits. This is the best possible outcome for an individual company.

COLLUSION AND GAME THEORY

If one company reduces its price to $2.50 per gallon, however, others will see their profits and sales fall. They are unlikely to keep prices at $4 per gallon. They will want to cut prices too. We would see a period of price competition during which prices fall back down to $2 per gallon and everyone ends up making low profits again. In this scenario, the collusion has broken down and the companies can no longer

make high profits. This is an example of game theory — the outcome of your choice depends on how rival companies react. If you cut prices, do you know how your rivals will respond?

OPEC

The Organization of the Petroleum Exporting Countries (OPEC) brings together the world's major oil producers. It often acts like a cartel to try to set oil prices. In the 1970s, OPEC restricted output and the price of oil tripled overnight. Oil producers made more profit, and oil importers faced higher prices. It was a classic example of a cartel maximizing profits for its members. However, OPEC was a victim of its own success.

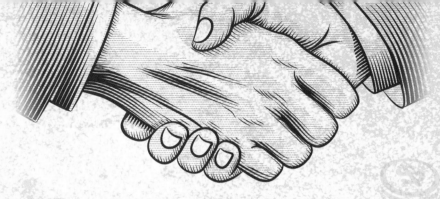

The high price encouraged oil importers to try to reduce demand (for example, the United States started developing more fuel-efficient cars). The high price also made it profitable to produce oil in new areas like Alaska, the North Sea and Venezuela. Over time, despite fluctuations, the increased supply caused the oil price to fall. Furthermore, OPEC's influence has been reduced by countries becoming less dependent on oil, by, for example, turning to gas-fired power stations.

Sometimes OPEC, and Saudi Arabia in particular, would try to increase price by restricting output. But often other countries would free-ride on Saudi Arabia's output restriction, and keep producing a high output. As a result, Saudi Arabia and core OPEC countries lost the ability to keep prices high. Since 2015, there is evidence that Saudi Arabia has tried a different strategy — keeping prices low to force rival countries (with higher costs of production) out of business.

PUNISHMENT FOR COLLUSION

In the United States and Europe there are high penalties for collusion. But the law offers protection to the first company that confesses and provides details of the collusion. Therefore, if you are colluding with another

company or companies, it may become a game of chicken. If you keep colluding, you make more profit. However, if a competitor confesses to the collusion, you are faced with a heavy fine and perhaps even a prison sentence. If you are the first to confess, then the collusion ends, but at least you don't have to pay a penalty.

How far would you trust a rival company? It is an unstable equilibrium because there is a strong incentive to be the first company to confess. That is exactly what government regulators hope to achieve — making collusion very unstable by setting a very high penalty if it is discovered.

▼ *Collusion is more profitable than competition. But, if you are colluding, there is incentive to be the firm that first confesses illegal behavior. If you collude and a rival firm confesses, you could go to jail. Therefore, collusion is unlikely to last.*

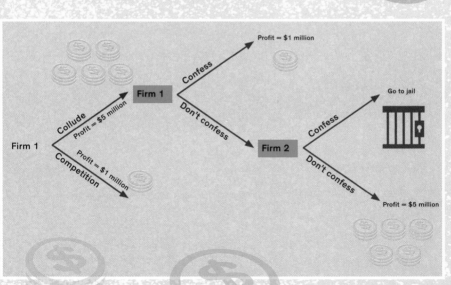

Profit = $1 million

Confess

Firm 1

Collude   Profit = $5 million

Don't confess

Firm 1

Competition   Profit = $1 million

Go to jail

Confess

Firm 2

Don't confess

Profit = $5 million

OBJECTIVES OF COMPANIES

In classical economics, we assume companies seek to maximize profits.

PROFIT MAXIMIZATION

Profit is desirable:

- It enables the founders and owners of a business to receive financial return in the form of higher salaries and dividends, and so on.
- It enables companies to invest and expand capacity.
- It can be saved to enable companies to survive economic downturns and protect jobs.
- It is easily measurable and a clear marker of success.

Is this too simplistic an assumption? Do companies always seek profit maximization? In fact, companies can be driven by different motivations.

▼ *The Amazon distribution center in Rheinberg, Germany.*

SALES MAXIMIZATION

Firms may seek to increase market share and sales above profit maximization. For example, Amazon has often stated that its primary aim is to increase market share, and it has often posted very low profits. In 2013, Amazon made $0.274 billion profit on sales of $74.45 billion. This is a tiny profit margin given Amazon's rapid growth. Amazon sells many goods at very low prices, encouraging people to use Amazon and creating long-term customers. Amazon will be able to maximize profits in the very long term if it can raise prices without losing customers.

ALTRUISTIC MOTIVES

Economics generally works from a principle of financial reward and incentives. But people may have altruistic motives that place the environment, charitable aims or social welfare before revenue and profit. For example, companies may avoid practices that damage the environment. Cooperatives are based on entirely different principles, aiming to share the proceeds of business with all stakeholders — consumers, owners and workers.

However, it could be argued that multinational companies use altruistic aims as clever marketing strategies. So, for example, not using "sweatshop labor" and adopting environmentally friendly strategies are efforts to improve the strength of a company's brand and therefore its long-term profitability.

Altruistic Motives

Sales max

Profit max

Ethics

Sometimes you can maximize profit and sales by being ethical

◀ Profit maximization may conflict with ethics. However, it is possible a well-marketed ethical stance can help improve a brand image, leading to greater sales and more profits.

CREATIVE DESTRUCTION

Creative destruction is a term used to express the fact that the forces of capitalism cause constant change. Old, inefficient companies close down, enabling new, more efficient companies to come to the fore.

The phrase was coined by the Austrian-born American economist Joseph Schumpeter (1883–1950). Ironically, Schumpeter derived his ideas from a reading of Karl Marx, who stated in *The Communist Manifesto* that capitalism went through different crises, when capital would be destroyed for capitalists to make profit from rebuilding.

For Schumpeter, this process of creative destruction was a natural and beneficial process, allowing constant renewal and responding to changing technology and changing consumer preferences.

> Capitalism ... is by nature a form or method of economic change and not only never is but never can be stationary ... The fundamental impulse that sets and keeps the capitalist engine in motion comes from the new consumers goods, the new methods of production or transportation, the new markets, the new forms of industrial organization that capitalist enterprise creates.
>
> Joseph Schumpeter
> *Capitalism, Socialism and Democracy*, 1942

Unemployed
train drivers

Unemployed train driver
gets a job driving a truck

▲ *A steam train (old technology) becomes outdated as it is superseded by new technology (trucks).*
Drivers of steam trains will lose their jobs, but the unemployed train driver can get work driving a truck.

We can see creative destruction all around us — for example, the CD, which caused the demise of vinyl factories and record players. Yet only a few years later, very profitable music companies were hit by the arrival of digital downloads. Without this creative destruction, we would be stuck with a static economy — primarily agrarian with no growth. Creative destruction may be seen as a justification for laissez-faire economics — because, for example, it implies that temporary unemployment is necessary for better jobs and higher incomes to be created.

However, critics argue that creative destruction is often used as a specious justification for allowing perfectly good industries to go out of business due to short-term difficulties. Furthermore, creative destruction is all very well for academics writing from a distance, but it can take many years for workers made redundant by creative destruction to be retrained and find new work. The rust belt areas of the United States and the former coal-mining communities in the United Kingdom, which suffer high unemployment and low wages, are a sign of the human cost of creative destruction. Moreover, we may regret the creative destruction of industries that had social benefits. For example, the rise of the automobile caused railways to decline, but it has led to increased congestion and pollution.

STATE SUPPORT OF INDUSTRY

Suppose an industry has become unprofitable and a major company is threatened with closure. What should the government do? Should it intervene, offering a subsidy or loan to prevent unemployment? Or should the government allow the company to close down? The arguments for creative destruction (see page 120) make a strong case for a laissez-faire approach to industry. However, there can be cases when government intervention is preferable.

In 2008–10, the U.S. automobile industry was severely hit by a slump in global demand, a rise in oil prices and a shift in demand to more (foreign-produced) fuel-efficient cars. Major U.S. carmakers racked up major losses, especially General Motors and Chrysler. There was a convincing case for nonintervention — in the face of oversupply, inefficient U.S. car production and a rising budget deficit, why should the U.S. government support a declining, unprofitable industry?

However, some facts in this case suggested a different approach. The slump in demand was related to a very deep recession (2008–2009) that was not expected to last. Also, U.S. carmakers had been hit particularly hard by higher oil

U.S. car industry losing money

Temporary global recession

Temporary rise in oil price

Temporary production of wrong car

◀ *In 2009, the U.S. car industry was losing money due to short-term factors — recession and oil prices. It wasn't necessarily a fatal structural change. By comparison, the bankruptcy of Borders bookstores in 2011 was a reflection of the long-term rise in mail-order and e-books.*

$80bn

$70bn
+ lower
unemployment

◀ *Government*
spent $80bn. it
received $70bn
back plus lower
unemployment.

Government

prices, which increased demand for more fuel-efficient foreign cars.

By late 2008, General Motors and Chrysler were close to bankruptcy, but rather than allowing them to go out of business, over the next four years the U.S. Treasury invested $80 billion in the U.S. car industry (mostly in General Motors). The bailout effectively nationalized the industry. An estimated 7.25 million jobs are dependent on the U.S. car industry, and would have been at risk from the bankruptcy of major companies like General Motors and Chrysler. The bailout also enabled U.S. carmakers to invest in shifting to more fuel-efficient, smaller cars.

By 2015, the U.S. car industry had recovered, creating an estimated half-a-million new jobs. The government sold its share of the companies it had effectively saved, recouping $70.5 billion of its

initial investment. In strict terms, the taxpayer lost $9.5 billion, but without the bailout, the cost to the economy, in jobs and declining output, could have been even greater. A bankruptcy in 2009, at the height of the great recession, would have been very damaging for employment, the economy and consumer confidence.

This shows that — in exceptional circumstances — a temporary government bailout can prevent a bankruptcy caused by short-term factors. Of course, the trick is knowing the difference between inevitable long-term decline and temporary short-term difficulties.

CHAPTER 5

CONCEPTS

PARADOX OF THRIFT

This states that individual decisions to increase saving during a recession can lead to lower gross domestic product (GDP). In a recession, people fear unemployment and loss of income, and they are likely to cut back on borrowing and nonessential purchases, saving more against the threat of lost income. From a personal point of view, this is a rational and understandable decision.

What happens if the majority of consumers decide to save more? If everyone increases saving and reduces spending, there will be a fall in aggregate demand. Overall spending declines because people are saving more. This leads to a recession, and companies make people redundant. The fear of recession can become self-fulfilling:

- There is a fear of recession.
- Individuals save more.
- Higher saving leads to lower consumption.
- Lower consumption leads to recession.
- Recession and unemployment lead to more saving.

John Maynard Keynes developed the concept of "paradox of thrift" during the Great Depression of the 1930s. He noted

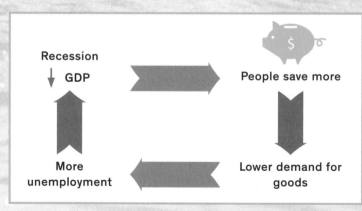

Recession
↓ GDP → People save more
↓
More unemployment ← Lower demand for goods

◄ *A recession causes people to save more and spend less. Less spending leads to more unemployment and a deeper recession*

▼ John Maynard Keynes.

▲ The Great Depression led to severe poverty for those out of work. There was a very human cost to this economic paradox.

that during this deep recession, the private sector cut back on investment and spending, and levels of saving rose. We saw this happen in 2008 too, when the recession caused a rapid rise in the savings ratio (percentage of income saved) and a fall in spending.

DEALING WITH THE PARADOX OF THRIFT

For Keynes, this rise in saving led to wasted resources — unemployment and unused capital. Keynes argued that if the private sector wouldn't spend, the public sector should intervene and spend. In a period of high private saving, the government should borrow and invest in the economy. Because savings were high, there would be demand for government bonds. In other words, government borrowing wouldn't "crowd out" the private sector, because there were unused savings.

IS SAVING ALWAYS BAD?

No! To confuse matters, higher saving is usually considered important for a successful economy in the long term. Higher saving enables banks to lend to companies to finance investment. In developing economies, it is often suggested that increasing the level of saving is important for enabling improved investment and economic development. Raising the long-run saving rates is also very important for the impending demographic time bomb (see Economics of an Aging Population, page 90).

MICRO AND MACRO DIFFERENCES

The paradox of thrift also explains a difference between micro- and macroeconomics. Microeconomics is concerned with individual transactions, like the decision made by an individual to save more. Macroeconomics looks at the whole economy — the effect of everyone saving more. The irony is that what makes sense for individuals can be harmful for the economy as a whole.

Suppose your wages increase by 10 percent — naturally, you think this is good news. But if everyone's wages increase by 10 percent because more money has been printed, and this leads to inflation of 10 percent, what looked like a wage increase doesn't leave you any better off.

CAN SAVING BE BAD?

The problem occurs if many consumers and businesses decide to increase savings (and reduce spending) all at the same time. It is this rapid rise in savings (and fall in spending) that can cause negative economic growth (see Economics of an Aging Population, page 90).

FALL IN THE SAVINGS RATIO

From the other perspective, a rapid fall in the savings ratio can be a warning sign that economic growth is unsustainable. If people increase spending by running down savings, this suggests the economic boom cannot be maintained in the long run. Before the crash of 2008, saving rates in the United Kingdom and United States had fallen to very low levels. It was a signal that the economy was unbalanced — leading to a spectacular correction.

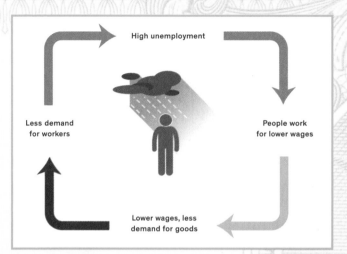

The paradox of toil suggests that if people respond to high unemployment by working for lower wages, the lower wages cause less demand for goods and therefore less demand for workers, therefore failing to solve unemployment.

High unemployment

People work for lower wages

Lower wages, less demand for goods

Less demand for workers

PARADOX OF TOIL

• • • • • • • • •

A similar concept is the paradox of toil. This states that in a period of deflation and zero interest rates, if everyone is desperate to work more at lower wages, this increase in labor supply pushes wages down and causes a fall in total demand.

LIFE-CYCLE HYPOTHESIS

This is the idea that individuals seek to smooth consumption over the course of their lives — "make hay while the sun is shining." In this case, while your income is higher than your lifetime average, save; while your income is lower than your lifetime average, borrow. As a student you build up debt; as a worker you earn and save; as a pensioner you run down your savings. This pattern of spending occurs partly out of necessity, but there is economic theory behind it.

If you want to train to be a doctor, you probably have no option but to take out student loans and go into debt. But you hope that by going into debt as a student you will be able to find a higher-paying job. By taking on student debt, you hope to increase your overall lifetime income.

Another reason to smooth income over a life cycle is the diminishing marginal utility of income. When you are earning a high salary (typically in your 40s), it can be hard to spend everything. If you already have one car, buying a second would bring only a relatively small increase in satisfaction. Therefore, it is more valuable to save this disposable income for your retirement, when you will have much lower income.

DO PENSIONERS DEPLETE SAVINGS?

Studies have found that many pensioners deplete their savings less than the model predicts. This is because pensioners tend to be risk-averse about unexpected expenses, such as health care or nursing homes. Also, pensioners

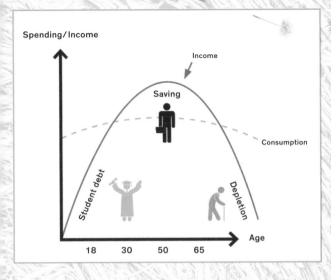

Spending/Income

Income

Saving

Consumption

Student debt

Depletion

Age

18   30   50   65

◀ *People aged 18–40 have a consumption that is greater than their income (they borrow money, e.g., student loans). At ages 40–65 people save for retirement. Consumption is less than their income. Those aged 65+ use wealth or savings to pay for retirement. Their consumption is greater than income.*

may be quite happy to leave their savings to their children.

IMPLICATIONS OF LIFE-CYCLE HYPOTHESES

The life-cycle hypothesis implies that consumer spending is not a simple function of income. If people have a sudden rise in income, they may not necessarily spend it. They may prefer to save for retirement. Milton Friedman developed a similar idea — the permanent income hypothesis, which claimed that people would spend at a level consistent with their expectations of a permanent income that can safely be spent. He argued that if the government pursued an expansionary fiscal policy (government spending more) and people saw a temporary increase in wages, they may not spend this extra income — because they would not be convinced it was a permanent increase in income.

LEISURE SMOOTHED OVER A LIFETIME

Another consideration is the different ways that the work–life balance may be approached over a lifetime. One option is to work very long hours between the ages of 21 and 50 and then take early retirement. But some people may prefer a job that enables them to work shorter hours, even if it means working to 70 and delaying retirement.

MULTIPLIER EFFECT

MULTIPLIER EFFECT
MULTIPLIER EFFECT
MULTIPLIER EFFECT

The multiplier effect states than an injection of money into the economy can have a bigger final impact because the rise in spending causes ripple effects. In other words, 10 + 1 = 11.5. We start by adding $1 billion of spending, but the multiplier effect means the final increase in output is $1.5 billion.

Suppose we have an economy with high levels of unemployment and the government decides to spend an extra $10 billion on building new roads. Unemployed workers now find employment and wages, and some companies see a rise in demand for raw materials. There is an increase of $10 billion in the economy and GDP could rise by $10 billion. However, the workers will also spend a part of their extra wages on other goods and services. Shops and bars in the area may see higher demand, and therefore higher profits. These companies and their workers have more money to spend, so the cycle of extra spending goes on. From the additional injection of $10 billion, the final increase in spending and GDP may be $17 billion — there is a multiplier effect of 1.7.

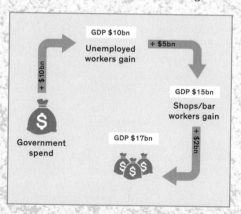

GDP $10bn

Unemployed workers gain

+ $5bn

+ $10bn

GDP $15bn

Shops/bar workers gain

Government spend

GDP $17bn

+ $2bn

◀ *If the government spends $10 billion, gross domestic product (GDP) increases by $10 billion. However, the investment causes unemployed workers to gain higher wages and they spend more of their extra income in shops and bars. This causes further rises in GDP. As people get more income, they spend more, spreading the benefits further around the economy.*

IS THERE A LIMIT TO THE MULTIPLIER EFFECT?

It seems this multiplier effect could cause ever-increasing demand. But there are various factors that limit it.

Tax. The government will take some of the increase in the form of income tax.

Saving. If workers and other income earners save the extra money, there will be no multiplier effect.

Imports. Spending on imports causes money to leave the economy.

Inflation and full capacity. If the government spends $10 billion when the economy is at full capacity, the extra spending may cause inflation. Additionally, the higher government spending may take resources from the private sector and so fail to increase overall output.

On the other hand, it may not just be about demand. During the Great Depression, the U.S. government built the Hoover Dam to provide work and boost demand. Sixty years later it is still providing energy and is part of the economy's productive capacity. The multiplier effect is biggest when there is unemployment, spare capacity (companies can increase productivity to optimal), and leakages (saving, imports, taxes) are low.

The multiplier effect explains why cities want to host the Olympic Games. There are many presumed benefits:

- Demand for hotels increases.
- Hotel workers earn overtime and spend more.
- Bars see more demand, and bar staff spend more on goods.
- Everyone in the local economy enjoys some degree of ripple effect from the increased spending.

MARGINAL PROPENSITY TO CONSUME

This is the amount of extra income that is spent. If you give a billionaire a 10 percent tax cut, he may spend only a small percentage of the extra income (there isn't much a billionaire needs!). Therefore, the marginal propensity to consume could be 0.1. However, if you cut taxes for low-income workers, they will probably spend a high percentage of this extra income, on goods they couldn't previously afford. These workers have a higher marginal propensity to consume.

NEGATIVE MULTIPLIER EFFECT

The multiplier effect can also work in the opposite direction.

Suppose a town's major employer closes down (for example, General Motors in Detroit, or effectively the entire coal-mining industry in the United Kingdom). Many workers are made redundant and their income falls dramatically. However, it is not just workers who are adversely affected. The newly unemployed will not be able to afford certain goods and services, and restaurants and bars in the town may also close down, causing

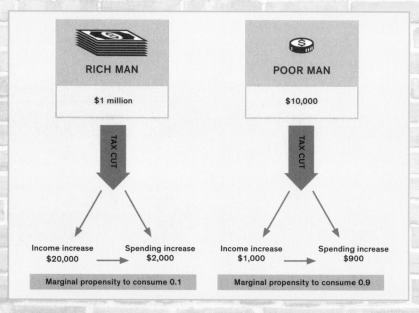

RICH MAN

$1 million

TAX CUT

Income increase
$20,000 → Spending increase
$2,000

Marginal propensity to consume 0.1

POOR MAN

$10,000

TAX CUT

Income increase
$1,000 → Spending increase
$900

Marginal propensity to consume 0.9

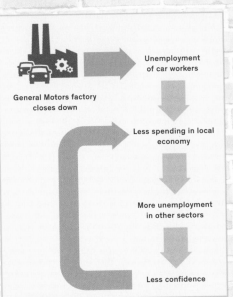

General Motors factory closes down → Unemployment of car workers

Less spending in local economy

More unemployment in other sectors

Less confidence

unemployment in related firms. If these job losses lead to a fall in confidence, businesses and young people may move away to more prosperous areas. If we are not careful, a whole town can be devastated by this negative cycle of falling demand and job losses.

GOVERNMENT INTERVENTION TO STOP NEGATIVE MULTIPLIER EFFECT

• • • • • • • • •

If a town's major employer closes down, it becomes difficult to stop this negative multiplier effect. The government could invest in new industries and new projects or move government jobs to the town to provide employment, and provide retraining for the unemployed workers to help them find new jobs.

◀ When a large steel factory closes down, it doesn't affect just steel workers but everyone living in that town. With steel workers unemployed, no money is spent, causing related businesses to close too. Formerly prosperous towns can become ghost towns.

LUDDITE FALLACY

The Luddite fallacy contends that labor-saving technology does not lead to higher overall unemployment in the economy. In other words, new technology doesn't destroy jobs — it only changes the composition of jobs in the economy (see Creative Destruction, page 120).

WHY PEOPLE THINK NEW TECHNOLOGY CAUSES UNEMPLOYMENT

In the United Kingdom in the 19th century, mechanized power looms were able to do the work of many skilled weavers. The development of these new machines caused many people to lose their livelihoods. Understandably, the newly unemployed workers blamed the new machines for the loss of their jobs. In desperation, some workers — known as "Luddites" — began smashing the machines in protest.

WHY NEW TECHNOLOGY DOESN'T CAUSE A RISE IN UNEMPLOYMENT

The new machines are more efficient, enabling clothes to be produced at a lower cost and sold at lower prices. If they buy cheaper clothes, consumers have more income to purchase other goods and services, and this increased demand may create new jobs. This new employment is less visible, but if we look at new technology, it has transformed the economy, leading to a growth in the leisure sector compared to 100 years ago.

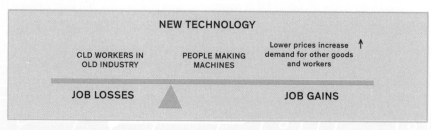

NEW TECHNOLOGY

OLD WORKERS IN OLD INDUSTRY | PEOPLE MAKING MACHINES | Lower prices increase demand for other goods and workers ↑

JOB LOSSES   JOB GAINS

▲ New technology causes job losses, but it also creates jobs — people making the machines and more efficient production enable higher demand for workers in new industries.

◀ *The loss of their jobs and livelihoods led to real poverty and suffering for the Luddite workers. Factory owners had to defend their businesses from protesting Luddites.*

UNEMPLOYMENT

However, new technology can cause some people to lose their jobs, at least in the short term. The plight of the "Luddites" was real. After the Napoleonic Wars of 1803–15, the UK economy was in recession, and there were fewer jobs available and wages were low.

At other times, there has been rapid technological change leading to job losses, but unemployed workers have been quickly absorbed by new industries. For example, the decline of the railways in the 1940s and 1950s was very rapid, but the car industry was growing even more rapidly, and workers could easily move across.

IS THE LUDDITE FALLACY ALWAYS A FALLACY?

For some workers, new technology can lead to long-term structural unemployment. For example, without effective retraining, unskilled manual laborers may be unable to find work in the new high-skilled service-sector industries.

If the U.S. car industry closes down, new jobs may be created in other industries like IT. The unemployed car workers may not have the right skills to work in IT, however, so remain unemployed.

New technology is unlikely to increase average long-term unemployment, but there may well be some people who lose out from the rapid introduction of new technology. There is no guarantee that the transition to new types of jobs will be smooth and painless.

MORAL HAZARD

Moral hazard is a concept that suggests individuals will take more risks if they feel they are insured against the consequences of risk-taking. If an insurance company agrees to insure your bike against theft, you may feel less incentive to take care of it — if your bike does get stolen, you will receive compensation.

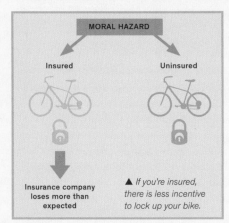

MORAL HAZARD

Insured | Uninsured

Insurance company loses more than expected

▲ *If you're insured, there is less incentive to lock up your bike.*

However, this kind of moral hazard is relatively easy to prevent. Insurance policies usually have a $50 excess, meaning that you pay the first $50 of any claim. Insurance may be dependent on certain actions — for example, your bike will not be insured if it is left unlocked. Furthermore, insurance companies make you go through a lot of paperwork and hassle to make a claim. Therefore, you

have a clear incentive to look after your bike, beyond the inconvenience of having it stolen.

MORAL HAZARD AND BANKING

A more serious case of moral hazard can be found in the banking sector. One of the biggest problems of the Great Depression of the 1930s was bank failures. Because banks went bust and people lost their savings, there was a collapse in confidence in the normal banking system. A similar situation occurred in 2008. To prevent the possibility of bankruptcy, governments and central banks have promised to act as the lender of last resort. They guarantee the savings of individuals and give savers more confidence. This encourages them to deposit money and prevents destabilizing bank runs.

However, if a central bank offers unconditional finance, banks know that if they get into trouble, they will be bailed out by the government. So there is an incentive for a bank to take risks. If the risk pays off, the bank makes more profit. If the risk doesn't pay off, the government will prevent it going bankrupt.

"TOO BIG TO FAIL"

"Too big to fail" is a measure of the banks' importance for the financial health of the economy. If banks are allowed to fail, the shock to confidence could lead to a serious recession. This means banks have a rare privilege and can rely on government intervention that wouldn't be given to companies in other sectors. In 2008, the U.S. Treasury allowed Lehman Brothers, a relatively small investment bank, to go out of business, but the repercussions on the financial markets were very serious and were a factor in deepening the credit crisis and the global economic downturn.

There have been calls for banks to split up their operations and separate ordinary savings accounts from risky investment-banking decisions. This means governments act as guarantors for the savings of individuals, but won't protect banks who undertake risky investment. However, in practice, it can be hard to separate out banking operations, and even allowing investment banks to fail could cause real financial hardship.

MORAL HAZARD AND THE CREDIT CRUNCH

• • • • • • • •

During the boom years of the early 21st century, banks in the United States took significant risks (see Housing Market, page 260). They issued so-called subprime mortgages that were profitable but risky. The people who ran the banks had an incentive to pursue this strategy, because they were entitled to big bonuses if they succeeded. But when house prices in the United States fell and mortgage defaults rose, banks around the world that had bought financial instruments derived from subprime mortgages started to lose money (see Credit Crunch, page 266). Many governments had to bail out banks that had taken on the subprime mortgage debt. The problem is that in the good years, banks were very profitable, but when the market turned they relied on taxpayer bailouts.

TRICKLE-DOWN ECONOMICS

Trickle-down theory claims that if the wealthy in society enjoy an increase in income then everybody benefits, because the wealth will trickle down to other people in the economy.

This is a justification for policies that increase incentives and lower taxes for wealthy businesspeople. The argument is that if the wealthy benefit from tax cuts, they will have more disposable income, leading to increased income for other businesses and workers in the economy. Furthermore, lower tax rates will enable more retained profit, which can lead to higher investment. This investment will in turn lead to increased employment and a positive multiplier effect in the economy. Therefore, everyone in the economy benefits.

The term "trickle-down economics" tends to be used by critics of laissez-faire and supply-side economics. These critics argue that economic policies that primarily benefit the rich have little benefit for the rest of the population.

U.S. President Ronald Reagan's supply-side economics of the 1980s was an example of trickle-down economics in action. The period saw lower income tax for the rich and widening inequality.

▶ *This is the theory of the trickle-down effect. If the rich get more wealth, everyone will benefit.*

Rich man

Middle class

Working class

Homeless

WHY IS THE TRICKLE-DOWN EFFECT WEAK?

First, there is a higher marginal propensity to save. If a millionaire receives a tax cut, they may spend only a small proportion of this extra income — they have a low marginal propensity to spend. Therefore, there is little increase in overall demand in the economy. Second, if the richest enjoy increased disposable income, they may save that money in tax havens and avoid paying tax. Third, increased income for the wealthy may lead to an asset bubble (overvalued shares or house prices), as they seek a destination for their increased income.

However, although it is widely used as a means of criticism, trickle-down theory is not without some justification. According to estimates by the U.S. Tax Policy Center, the top 1 percent of Americans paid 45.7 percent of individual income taxes in 2014. Therefore, higher income for top earners does enable higher government spending. But while increasing the wealth of the rich does appear to have a positive ripple effect, it is probably not the most efficient way to improve the living standards of the poor.

HORSE-AND-SPARROW THEORY

• • • • • • • • • • • • • • • • • •

The Canadian-born American economist John Kenneth Galbraith (1908–2006) described trickle-down theory in rather unglamorous terms: "If you feed the horse enough oats, some will pass through to the road for the sparrows." Galbraith claimed this horse-and-sparrow theory was behind the inequality of the Gilded Age and even partly to blame for the U.S. economic depression known as the Panic of 1896.

LAFFER CURVE

The Laffer curve plots a relationship between tax rates (0 percent to 100 percent) and overall tax revenue. It suggests that if you cut high rates of income tax, you can increase overall tax revenue. As you may expect, this is very politically appealing — if lower taxes mean more revenue, everyone is happy! The argument was popularized by American economist Arthur Laffer (b. 1940), who drew the Laffer curve on the back of a napkin during a meeting in 1974 with officials from President Gerald Ford's administration.

The argument is that if you have an income tax rate of 100 percent, you will raise zero revenue. In other words, people won't work if every cent they earn goes in tax revenue. Similarly, if the tax rate is 0 percent, the revenue raised would also be zero. Therefore, there should be some point in the middle that represents the optimal tax rate for maximizing revenue.

If income tax rates were very high, at 80 percent, and the government cut them to 70 percent, it is possible that the government would see an increase in tax revenue. The fall in income tax rates

▼ *The Laffer curve plots the idea that increasing the income tax rate above a certain level can lead to less tax revenue.*

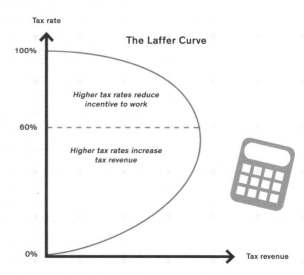

The Laffer Curve

Tax rate

100%

Higher tax rates reduce incentive to work

60%

Higher tax rates increase tax revenue

0%

Tax revenue

encourages more people to work and overall tax revenue increases — even though the average income tax bill falls. Unfortunately, even with income tax rates of 40–50 percent for top earners, there is little evidence that cutting the tax rate increases income tax revenue. The shape of the Laffer curve is uncertain and disputed, but some have suggested a rate of 70 percent may be the optimal tax rate (if the goal was maximizing total income tax revenue). Moreover, the optimal tax rate could also change over time.

Despite its limitations, the idea behind the Laffer curve complemented the ideological push that drove the supply-side economics of the 1980s, and, in particular, Ronald Reagan's supply-side reforms, which had income tax cuts as a key economic policy.

Under Reagan, the top marginal income tax rate fell from 70.1 percent in 1981 to 28.4 percent in 1986. This was a very big cut in income tax, but the budget deficit rose from 2.6 percent of GDP in 1981 to 6 percent in 1983 — there was no miraculous increase in tax revenue (though of course other factors were at play, such as the 1981 recession, which led to a cyclical fall in tax revenue).

▲ Reagan's economic policies broke with the postwar consensus. Reagan is associated with supply-side economics and free-market reforms such as tax cuts and deregulation.

VOODOO ECONOMICS

Back in 1980, George H.W. Bush famously called supply-side economics — the claim that tax cuts miraculously increase tax revenues — "voodoo economics." Bush later regretted saying this, but many critics argue that large tax cuts are not a magic bullet for boosting economic productivity, but can increase levels of inequality.

18

In 1982 and 1984, Reagan had to institute tax-raising measures. This involved broadening the tax base, closing tax loopholes and reducing tax breaks; he also increased social security taxes. The average federal tax receipt in the Reagan years was 18.2 percent of GDP, which was close to the 40-year average of 18.1 percent. So Reagan's reputation as a tax cutter is more complex than the headline cut in income tax revenues suggests.

The Reagan years were an experiment in cutting income tax rates, but evidence of rising income tax revenues is hard to find. Some economists are dubious that the Laffer curve has any real usefulness for tax policy, beyond stating the obvious — that extremely high income tax rates can be self-defeating. And it is important to bear in mind that, when setting income tax rates, there are many aims beyond the question of which rate maximizes income tax revenue. These aims include equality, fairness, impact on incentives to work, and so on.

ARTHUR LAFFER

Arthur Laffer pointed out that the ideas behind his Laffer curve could be found as far back as the 14th century, when the North African philosopher Ibn Khaldun noted in the Muqaddimah: "It should be known that at the beginning of the dynasty, taxation yields a large revenue from small assessments. At the end of the dynasty, taxation yields a small revenue from large assessments."

ON THE OTHER HAND

**U.S. President Harry Truman once remarked in exasperation, "Give me a one-handed economist … All my economists say, 'on the one hand … on the other.'"
Why do economists so frequently talk about "the other hand"?**

Many things cannot be predicted with certainty. If we talk about the effect of higher income tax, one argument states that this will raise revenue for the government. On the other hand, it is possible that higher taxes will discourage people from working and tax revenue will increase less than forecast.

Just because something happened in the past, doesn't mean it will happen again. For example, in normal circumstances the decision by a central bank to increase the money supply will cause inflation. On the other hand, in special circumstances (for example, liquidity trap or recession), increasing the money supply may not increase inflation.

IT'S NOT A BLACK-AND-WHITE WORLD

• •

It may be frustrating for Truman that economists hedged their advice, but we don't live in a black-and-white world. "On the other hand" means we are able to see the situation from another perspective. Even if we don't agree with the opposite point of view (e.g., cutting taxes), it is good to be aware there is another side of the argument. A good economist should avoid fundamentalism and a simplistic, biased viewpoint.

Human behavior is not always rational or predictable. Economic theory often starts from the principle that consumer behavior is rational, and therefore, for example, higher prices will reduce demand. On the other hand, what about the higher prices of designer clothes that makes them more attractive to some consumers who want to show off their wealth? This may not be rational but it does happen (see Veblen Goods, page 40).

Because economists are judged by the accuracy of their forecasts, they may hedge their bets. If you look back at 2008, you will find economists saying that there was no prospect of recession. But we know the economy did go into recession.

So if you are making a prediction, it is safer to say, "Given the current situation, recession is unlikely. On the other hand, if the fall in confidence continues, there could be a recession."

The main issue is that there are nearly always conflicting forces at work in an economy and economists do not have enough information to know which factors will prove the strongest. This is both the fascination and the frustration of economics. Outcomes are nearly always uncertain. In the real world, it is impossible to isolate the innumerable variables.

IRRATIONAL EXUBERANCE

Irrational exuberance describes a situation that sees overeager buyers push up the price of assets beyond their fundamental value.

For example, we would expect share values to have some relation to profits and earnings, but the dot-com bubble of the late 1990s saw the share prices of IT companies rise much more rapidly than profits before the market crashed and many companies were declared bankrupt. Irrational exuberance is a polite way of talking about the folly of people who get carried away by a booming market. It was coined by the American economist and Chairman of the Federal Reserve Alan Greenspan (b. 1926) in a 1996 speech, "The Challenge of Central Banking in a Democratic Society," which he gave at the beginning of the dot-com bubble. What are the factors that cause irrational exuberance?

"The wisdom of crowds." If everyone else is buying shares or houses, we think they must know something, and it is easy to be caught up in this widespread enthusiasm for buying. Being swept along by majority opinion is sometimes less kindly referred to as "collective insanity."

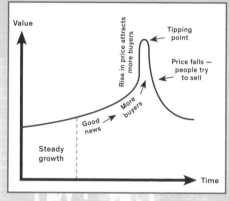

▲ *Price rises at a rapid rate until the irrational exuberance switches to abject pessimism.*

Past success. A powerful motivation for believing in the future success of an asset is the fact that we have made money from it in the past. If we have seen our house value increase for the past 10 years, it feels like a very good investment and this can give an optimism bias for the future.

Security and stability. Booms often occur during a period of economic stability — a period of strong economic growth, low inflation and low unemployment. This macroeconomic stability can give the impression that everything is stable and secure. The dot-com bubble took place against the backdrop of a seemingly stable economy, as did the housing bubble of the early 2000s.

This time it is different. The U.S.-born British investor John Templeton (1912–2008) said that, "The four most expensive words in the English language are, 'This time it's different.' " Sometimes, when assets become divorced from traditional valuations (for example, price or earnings), some people will still find reasons to think that this time it will be different. For example, if the ratio of house prices to earnings rises above the long-term trend, some people may prefer to believe that this is because of a housing shortage and the greater availability of mortgages — and not because house prices have become dangerously overinflated. In the case of the dot-com bubble, some internet companies did see unprecedented growth, and this provides grounds for ignoring the usual trends in the profit-to-share-price ratio.

THE SOUTH SEA BUBBLE OF 1720

• •

The South Sea bubble was a period when shares in the South Sea Company became wildly inflated in a short period of time. People bought into the rising prices hoping to make a quick profit. But shares became vastly overvalued, and after a tipping point they plunged back to a fairer value.

In the spring of 1720, Isaac Newton sold his shares in the South Sea Company, successfully doubling his money. Speaking of the irrational exuberance surrounding the South Sea Bubble, Newton said:

> I can calculate the movement of the stars, but not the madness of men.
>
> Isaac Newton

DIMINISHING RETURNS

Increasing a certain input factor of production leads to smaller and smaller improvement in total output — a diminishing return. Note, however, that output doesn't fall, but increases at a slower rate.

If you have ever tried to stay up all night, cramming for an exam the next morning, you will probably be aware of diminishing returns. The first hour of study is the most productive because you are fresh and keen. But by the seventh hour, the gain in knowledge is much smaller — because you are tired and bored, it is harder to remember new facts. Studying for a seventh hour does improve your knowledge, but at a lower rate. Because of this diminishing return, it would be more efficient to spend two hours studying every day, rather than do nothing for a week and then cram in eight hours on the last night (though many of my own students swear cramming is the only way to get through!).

DIMINISHING RETURNS ON LABOR

At a certain point, employing extra workers produces a decline in productivity. If you own a small restaurant, employing one worker may allow you to serve eight customers per hour. Employing a second worker may help boost productivity because it is more efficient for one worker to cook

LEARNING CURVE

If you spend time in an industry, you gradually learn more efficient methods of production and ways of working. If you take a job such as teaching, at the start you may face a steep learning curve. In the first few years, the experience helps to make you more effective at your job. However, as time passes, the improvement in learning and skills increases at a slower rate. In other words, we usually get diminishing returns on learning.

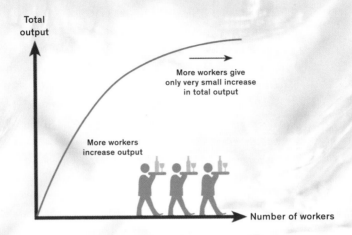

Total output

More workers give
only very small increase
in total output

More workers
increase output

Number of workers

and one to act as a waiter. Employing two workers may enable you to serve a total of 20 customers. However, if it is a small restaurant, there will come a point at which extra workers yield smaller increases in sales. The fifth and sixth workers may have low marginal productivity, and help serve only a few extra customers.

WHY DO WE GET DIMINISHING RETURNS?

In other words, why do too many cooks spoil the broth? If you have one person responsible for managing a restaurant, they can get a lot done. If you employ two managers, they may spend time arguing about the best way forward, and the improvement in productivity

will be limited. If you employ a third manager to oversee the restaurant, workers may become annoyed at the constant scrutiny and be confused by contradictory instructions. If you employ more workers than can comfortably fit in your restaurant, they may end up lining up for access to the work stations and stoves. Essentially, extra workers start to get in the way. They may help a bit, but are much less productive than the first few workers.

However, if we can increase capital or, for example, move to larger premises, then it is possible to increase staff without diminishing returns.

HYSTERESIS

Hysteresis suggests that past events will affect the future. Hysteresis usually refers to the fact that a sudden rise in unemployment (due to, for example, demand-side shock) may lead to a permanent rise in long-term unemployment, even after initial causes have subsided.

The logic for hysteresis is as follows. If people are made redundant during a recession, it will be harder for them to find new jobs in the future because they are less attractive to employers — they lose on-the-job training and don't keep up with latest trends. Also, if workers are made redundant, they may become demotivated and pessimistic about their chances of future employment.

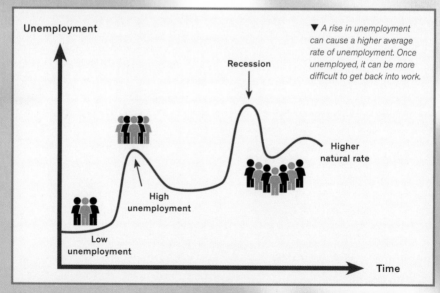

▼ A rise in unemployment can cause a higher average rate of unemployment. Once unemployed, it can be more difficult to get back into work.

Unemployment

Recession

Higher natural rate

High unemployment

Low unemployment

Time

▲ *Recession causes unemployment to rise, but recessions and the rise in unemployment also cause the average unemployment rate to rise.*

Often when the economy recovers and economic growth restarts, the unemployment rate takes time to start to fall — suggesting that the hysteresis effect is in effect. For example, after the recessions of the 1970s and early 1980s, the natural rate of unemployment in the United States and the United Kingdom rose.

However, some people argue that the hysteresis effect is very limited. If labor markets are flexible, there is no reason why somebody who is unemployed cannot get a job during an economic recovery. The reasons for higher average unemployment rates are more complex than just hysteresis effects. After the 2008–2009 recession, unemployment in United Kingdom and the United States. fell relatively quickly — very different to from the 1981–1982 recession.

CHAPTER 6

MACROECONOMICS

INFLATION

Inflation means a sustained increase in prices, causing a rise in the cost of living and a decline in the value of money. Or as baseball player Sam Ewing put it, "Inflation is when you pay fifteen dollars for the ten-dollar haircut you used to get for five dollars when you had hair." Does it matter if inflation is high and prices are rising rapidly? Well, there are several problems associated with high inflation.

If you hold cash, inflation reduces the value of your savings. As prices rise, your cash savings buy fewer goods. Suppose you bought a 10-year government bond for $1,000 in 1971. Between 1971 and 1981, the United States had a cumulative inflation rate of 124 percent. Adjusted for inflation, your $1,000 bond should be worth $2,244.44 in 1981. But in 1981, when the government redeems your bond, you get back only $1,000. With $1,000 you can buy fewer goods in 1981 than in 1971. Inflation has reduced the value of your savings.

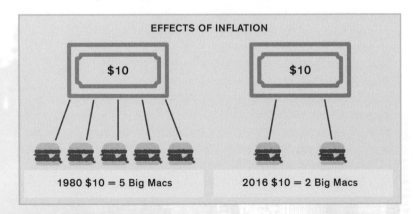

EFFECTS OF INFLATION

$10

$10

1980 $10 = 5 Big Macs

2016 $10 = 2 Big Macs

▲ *Since 1980, inflation has led to a steady rise in prices and a decline in the value of money. In 1980, $10 bought five Big Macs, but in 2016, $10 buys only two Big Macs.*

It's not quite as bad as it sounds. In 1971 the interest rate on bonds was 6.24 percent. Including all interest payments, the bond is worth $1,863.36 in 1981, but this is still less than the real value. Buying a government bond was better than keeping cash under the mattress. But because inflation turned out to be higher than the interest rate, the saver who bought bonds in 1971 lost out.

Inflation made it easier for the government and companies to pay off their debts. This is convenient for the government, but not so good for savers. And if the rate of inflation is allowed to rise, savers will not want to buy government bonds — unless there is a very high interest rate.

> By a continuing process of inflation, government can confiscate, secretly and unobserved, an important part of the wealth of their citizens.
>
> John Maynard Keynes

IS INFLATION ALWAYS BAD?

If your wages rise faster than inflation, your effective purchasing power will still increase. Suppose your wages increase by 7 percent, and inflation stands at 5 percent — your real wage will have increased by 2 percent. Similarly, if the interest rate you receive from a bank is higher than the inflation rate, you will protect the real value of your savings. Finally, a moderate amount of inflation is often a necessary consequence of economic growth. Central banks usually try to maintain inflation at 2 percent — rather than targeting inflation of 0 percent. But inflation of 5 percent and higher can cause real economic costs.

CAUSES OF INFLATION

What economic conditions cause companies to increase prices?

DEMAND-PULL INFLATION
This occurs during a period of rapid economic growth when aggregate demand grows faster than the productive capacity of the economy. In simple terms, companies can't keep pace with rising demand, so they respond by putting up prices. Demand-pull inflation can be caused by an increase in the money supply, rising wages or rising confidence. In the late 1980s and early 1990s, the United States saw a rise in inflation due to a booming economy.

INFLATION EXPECTATIONS
One of the best guides to predicting

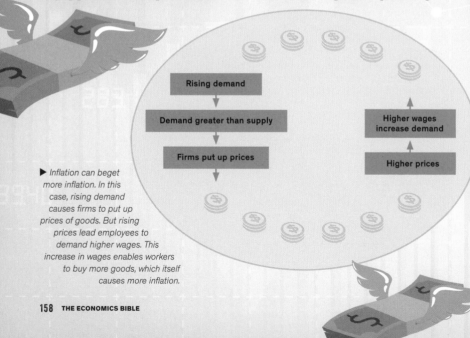

Rising demand

Demand greater than supply

Firms put up prices

Higher wages increase demand

Higher prices

▶ *Inflation can beget more inflation. In this case, rising demand causes firms to put up prices of goods. But rising prices lead employees to demand higher wages. This increase in wages enables workers to buy more goods, which itself causes more inflation.*

inflation is to look at the inflation during the current year. If inflation is high, it tends to be high the next year as well. If inflation is low, it is much easier to keep it low. This is because expectations of future inflation are important. If people expect high inflation, companies will put up prices in anticipation of rising costs, and workers will demand higher wages in anticipation of rising living costs. Therefore, inflation becomes self-fulfilling:

- There is an expectation of inflation.
- Companies put up prices and workers bargain for higher wages.
- This causes the expected inflation.

COST-PUSH INFLATION

This is caused by a rise in the cost of production rather than rising demand. For example, if oil prices rise, we see higher transport costs, which will be passed on to consumers in the form of higher prices.

The 1970s saw rising global inflation because of higher oil prices. The cost-push inflation also led to higher wages as workers tried to maintain the level of their real wages.

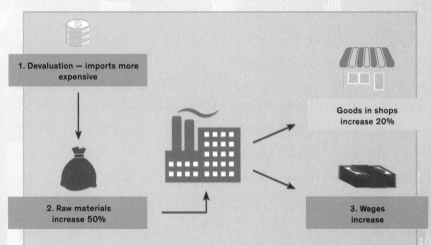

1. Devaluation — imports more expensive

2. Raw materials increase 50%

Goods in shops increase 20%

3. Wages increase

▲ *Devaluation can cause inflation. It causes a rising price of imported raw materials. Higher manufacturing costs cause firms to put up prices.*

PRINTING MONEY

Governments and central banks have the capacity to print money. Therefore, there can be a temptation to print more money in response to shortages.

But what happens if you print more money? If a government doubles the money supply (the amount of money in circulation), this would, all things being equal, lead to higher prices. The quantity of goods would be the same, but with more money in the economy, companies would just increase prices.

Suppose a government prints $100 million of money. Its economy produces 10 million widgets costing $10 each, so the value of the economy is $100 million. If the government doubles the money supply to $200 million, we would still have 10 million widgets. People have more money, but the number of widgets doesn't change. If you have more money, you want to buy more goods, which causes prices to rise. But companies can't suddenly produce more widgets just because the government has printed more money. If the money supply is doubled, the most likely scenario is that we would have 10 million widgets costing $20 each. The economy is now worth $200 million rather than $100 million. There is an increase in nominal GDP, but the quantity of goods is exactly the same.

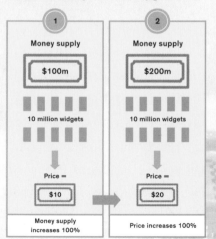

1	2
Money supply	Money supply
$100m	$200m
10 million widgets	10 million widgets
Price =	Price =
$10	$20
Money supply increases 100%	Price increases 100%

◀ *Doubling the money supply does nothing to alter the number of widgets. If there is more money and the same quantity of goods, we will just get a rise in the price of widgets.*

We can say that the increase in nominal GDP is a money illusion. True, you have 100 percent more money, but if everything is 100 percent more expensive, you are no better off. In this simple model, printing money has made goods more expensive but hasn't changed the quantity of goods.

PRINTING MONEY DOESN'T ALWAYS CAUSE INFLATION!

Just to complicate matters, in some circumstances it is possible to increase the money supply without causing inflation. During the prolonged economic downturn of 2008–16, the United States and the United Kingdom. pursued a policy of quantitative easing (see page 214) — and increasing the money supply (see page 20). However, due to depressed demand and a weak banking sector, this increase in the monetary base didn't lead to a significant increase in bank lending or spending, and the rate of inflation continued to fall.

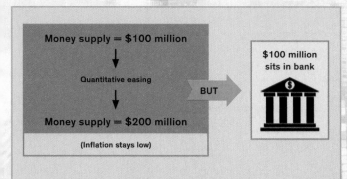

Money supply = $100 million

↓

Quantitative easing

↓

Money supply = $200 million

(Inflation stays low)

BUT

$100 million sits in bank

◀ *Quantitative easing could cause an increase in the money supply from $100m to $200m, but if $100m of this extra new money just stays in bank reserves, it will not cause inflation. This is a simplification, but it explains why inflation stayed low despite the efforts of the central banks.*

HYPERINFLATION

Hyperinflation is a very high and destabilizing rate of inflation — inflation of 100 percent or more. It can occur when a country responds to an economic crisis by printing more money. This usually creates a dynamic of ever-increasing prices and a need to keep printing more money.

GERMAN HYPERINFLATION

After the First World War, Germany had large war debts exacerbated by the Versailles Treaty, which demanded reparations in foreign currency. The debts caused the German deutsche mark to fall in value, and to meet the reparation payments Germany printed more deutsche marks in order to buy foreign currency. This caused a further devaluation in the deutsche mark and more inflation. The deutsche mark devalued from 8 deutsche marks per dollar in 1918 to 320 deutsche marks per dollar in 1922. By November 1923, one dollar was worth one trillion deutsche marks.

The falling deutsche mark meant more deutsche marks were needed to pay reparations. This encouraged the government to print more money, which caused higher inflation. It was a vicious cycle. In 1923, the economic crisis led to a major industrial strike, and, fearing unemployment and a potential communist revolution, the government printed more money in order to pay the striking workers. But this added more fuel to the hyperinflation and prices spun out of control.

▲ *The visible impact of hyperinflation. Huge quantities of nearly worthless money makes ordinary transactions increasingly difficult.*

Why didn't Germany act to stop hyperinflation? The German government could have stopped hyperinflation by halting the printing of money, but this would have caused workers to receive insufficient wages and companies would have gone bankrupt.

▲ Under hyperinflation, coins would be worthless unless the metal had some intrinsic value.

COSTS OF HYPERINFLATION

Many middle-class people saw their savings wiped out. Walter Levy, a German-born American, remembers that his father "had taken out an insurance policy in 1903, and every month he had made the payments faithfully. It was a 20-year policy, and when it became due, he cashed it in and bought a single loaf of bread." Hyperinflation changed the rules of society. People who had worked hard, were frugal and had saved saw their wealth wiped out. Hyperinflation created shock and mystification about how it could have happened.

As soon as people received cash, they would buy any goods they possibly could — preferably gold, food or jewelry. But at the height of hyperinflation, people would buy useless items like hairpins — anything, rather than end up with money, which would soon become worthless. As money became worthless, the barter economy became more important — a couple of eggs would buy a haircut. But not everyone lost out from hyperinflation. People with large debts could now easily pay them pay back, and wealthy industrialists with material resources were protected.

The hyperinflation was solved by bringing in a completely new currency, the Rentenmark, but people's savings were never recovered, and the experience created a deep sense of unease and suspicion.

DEFLATION

Deflation means a negative inflation rate — a fall in prices, which means that the value of money increases.

It doesn't matter if you hoard cash under your mattress, because in the future it will buy more goods and services. Although most economies target low inflation, many economists will tell you that the only thing worse than inflation is deflation. In many respects this sounds counterintuitive. After all, if prices fall — isn't that a good thing?

> If inflation is the genie, then deflation is the ogre that must be fought decisively.
> Christine Lagarde, Managing Director of the International Monetary Fund (IMF)

GOOD DEFLATION
First, if you have rising incomes and falling prices, deflation can be a good thing. During 1870–90, the United States experienced a period known as the Great Deflation, with moderate price falls caused by improved technology. This deflation was consistent with rising incomes and economic growth.

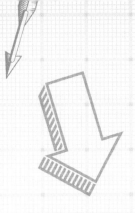

1908 average car $2,000

Henry Ford assembly line

1913 Model T $700

Lower prices for consumer

▶ In 1908, cars were made by hand in small units and were expensive to produce. Henry Ford's assembly line dramatically reduced the cost of producing cars because it was so much more efficient. Ford car prices fell dramatically to $700.

However, deflation can often cause serious macroeconomic problems. If prices are falling in the economy, it can lead consumers to delay buying expensive items. If you believe that a widescreen TV will be 10 percent cheaper next year, there is an incentive to put off buying it. But if lots of consumers start delaying their purchases, aggregate demand falls and companies struggle to sell goods. This can cause them to further cut prices in order to sell excess supply, causing more deflation.

In the 1990s and 2000s, Japan had a prolonged experience of deflation, which created very conservative consumers. Consumers became very frugal — and the search for cheaper prices became embedded in Japanese culture. In the face of such a mindset, it became very difficult to boost consumer spending and economic growth.

Second, there are many individuals and companies with significant levels of debt. Deflation makes it harder to pay this debt back. Falling prices tend to mean falling incomes and falling wages, so in a period of deflation people find they are paying a higher percentage of their income in debt repayments. This is particularly a problem for people who assume there will be a moderate rate of inflation when they take on debt.

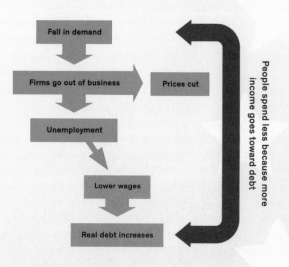

▲ A deflationary spiral. Lower demand causes unemployment, lower wages, rising debt. This feeds back to further falls in demand and falling prices.

EUROZONE DEFLATION

Falling demand puts pressure on firms to cut prices. Falling prices increase the real value of debt, making debtors worse off. This feeds back into lower demand. It is known as a deflationary spiral.

Debt deflation has been a real problem for many Eurozone economies. Falling prices and wages have caused lower consumer spending as servicing debt becomes a bigger burden. Debt deflation is also a problem for government debt. Falling prices can lead to a fall in nominal GDP, causing government debt-to-GDP ratios to rise.

Deflation can also lead to a phenomenon known as real-wage unemployment. Generally, workers try to resist nominal wage cuts — no one likes to see a fall in their wages. But if prices are falling, then effectively we see a rise in real wages. Therefore, in a period of deflation, labor can become more expensive and lead to a lower demand for labor.

▼ *The human cost of deflation. People out of work due to insufficient demand.*

DEFLATION IN THE GREAT DEPRESSION

• • • • • • • • • •

During the Great Depression, prices fell at a record level — 10 percent in 1931 in the United States. With low confidence in the banks, deflation encouraged people to save cash rather than spend. Moreover, there was little incentive to borrow. Deflation was a significant factor in prolonging the length of the recession.

UNEMPLOYMENT

Unemployment has very high economic and social costs. It is a major cause of poverty and can lead to depression, ill health, homelessness and bankruptcy. When unemployment is high, the wider economy also suffers from lost output, inefficient use of resources and lower tax revenue for the government.

WHAT CAUSES UNEMPLOYMENT?

In a recession, companies see falling demand, and therefore produce less and need fewer workers. Some companies will go out of business, leading to redundancies. As unemployment rises, there is a further fall in demand because those who have lost their jobs have less money to spend.

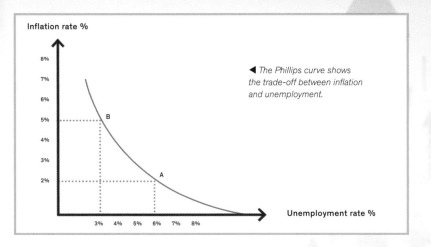

Inflation rate %

◀ *The Phillips curve shows the trade-off between inflation and unemployment.*

Unemployment rate %

PHILLIPS CURVE

Described by New Zealand economist William Phillips (1914–75), the Phillips curve suggests that there is a trade-off between unemployment and inflation. If true, it means policymakers can choose between reducing unemployment at the cost of more inflation, or reducing inflation at the cost of higher unemployment.

At point A, we have unemployment of 6 percent and inflation of 2 percent — there is low growth and high unemployment. If the central bank cuts interest rates, we would see more demand in the economy, and greater demand for goods would lead to more demand for labor, reducing unemployment. However, as we get closer to full employ-

ment, prices and nominal wages would rise, leading to inflation at point B. This is the trade-off — lower unemployment but higher inflation.

If demand falls, unemployment rises. High unemployment means workers will be willing to work for lower wages to try to get jobs.

There have been times when the Phillips curve seems to have reflected what is happening in the economy. For example, in the early 1980s the U.S. Federal Reserve reduced inflation, but at the cost of higher unemployment. Then, in the late 1980s, unemployment fell, but inflation rose as the economy grew rapidly. This suggests that there is a trade-off, at least in the short term.

CRITICISMS OF THE PHILLIPS CURVE

If there are higher oil prices (as in 1973–74), this causes cost-push inflation, but unemployment also rises due to the economic downturn. In this case, inflation and higher unemployment occur at the same time.

SUPPLY-SIDE POLICIES

Others argue that increasing demand leads to only a temporary fall in unemployment. To reduce unemployment in the long term we should concentrate on supply-side policies to reduce the natural rate of unemployment. These other causes of unemployment include:

Structural unemployment. Individual workers may be unemployed because they lack suitable skills and education. An unemployed manual worker from a steel factory may struggle to gain employment in new service-sector industries like IT. Even in a period of economic growth and "full capacity," some workers can be left in unemployment.

Real-wage unemployment. This is unemployment caused by rising wages — for example, a national minimum wage of $15 an hour may lead to a fall in labor demand.

Inflexible labor markets. Relatively high rates of unemployment in the European Union are often blamed on overprotective labor-market regulations (for example, a maximum working week, minimum hours, and the difficulty of firing workers), which discourage companies from employing workers in the first place.

BUDGET DEFICIT

The budget deficit is the annual amount the government needs to borrow from the private sector. It is the shortfall between government spending and tax revenues.

CYCLICAL DEFICIT

In a recession, government borrowing increases for various reasons.

- Fewer people working means lower income tax revenue.
- Lower consumer spending means lower sales tax revenue.
- Lower company profit means lower corporation tax revenue.

Furthermore, higher unemployment and poverty lead to increased government spending on entitlement welfare benefits.

AUTOMATIC STABILIZERS

This rise in the budget deficit during a recession acts as an automatic stabilizer. This is because a downturn that sees falling economic growth means that the government automatically reduces tax collection and increases spending, for example in welfare payments to the unemployed. The increased government spending helps to offset the fall in private-sector spending.

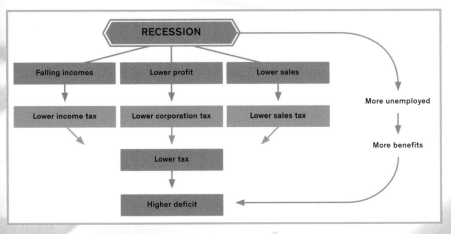

▲ *After the 2008–2009 recession, there was a rapid rise in budget deficits in both U.S. and EU economies. The negative growth saw a fall in income tax revenues and a need to spend more on unemployment benefits.*

In a period of rapid economic growth, the opposite happens — tax receipts rise and entitlement spending should fall.

STRUCTURAL DEFICIT

The structural deficit is the level of government borrowing that occurs even when the economy is at full employment. A structural deficit can occur for various reasons.

Demographic changes. A country like Japan has an aging population, which leads to higher spending on health care and pensions and relatively lower tax revenues. This is a factor behind the upward pressure on debt ratios in many Western economies.

Political difficulty of raising taxes. Politicians tend to get elected on promises of "no new taxes" and increased spending on popular public services such as health care. This can make it difficult for governments to agree on deficit-reducing policies.

Public investment. Like a company investing in new technology, a government may borrow to improve transport and education and build new housing.

Generally, a structural deficit is considered a more serious problem because you cannot necessarily rely on economic growth to reduce it.

NATIONAL DEBT

National debt is the total amount the government borrows by selling bonds and securities. It is the cumulative debt a government has acquired over years of budget deficits.

HOW DO GOVERNMENTS FINANCE GOVERNMENT DEBT?

Governments sell bonds to the private sector (for example, banks and pension funds). A government may sell a bond for $1,000 on which it pays an annual interest rate of 5 percent. At the end of the term (say 30 years), the government will also pay back the $1,000. Investors like to buy government bonds because they receive an annual interest dividend on their asset. Moreover, government bonds are seen as one of the most secure forms of saving — Western governments rarely default on their debts. However, if inflation is higher than the interest rate on bonds, savers will lose out.

$ 1 9 , 4 8 1 ,

HOW MUCH CAN A GOVERNMENT BORROW?

The figures for national debt can be staggering. In the United States, at the end of 2016, the estimated level of gross U.S. federal debt was $19 trillion or, even more dramatically, $19,481,571,141,221.67.

The size of these figures can be overwhelming. However, to understand debt, it is helpful to view it as a percentage of GDP.

Blessed are the young, for they shall inherit the national debt.

U.S. President Herbert Hoover addressing the Nebraska Republican Conference, Lincoln, Nebraska, January 16, 1936

5 7 1 , 1 4 1 , 2 2 1 . 6 7

COMPARISON OF NATIONAL DEBT BY COUNTRIES

••••

According to the CIA's 2015 *World Factbook*, countries rank globally as follows when public debt is given as a percentage of GDP:

1. Japan: 227.9 percent
3. Greece: 171.3 percent
5. Italy: 135.8 percent
17. Canada: 98.6 percent
25. UK: 90.6 percent
28. EU: 86.8 percent
39. U.S.: 73.6 percent
45. Germany: 71.7 percent
118. Norway: 39.3 percent
173. Saudi Arabia: 7.8 percent
177. Libya: 6.7 percent

This reveals a large variation in levels of government debt. A country like Saudi Arabia can easily raise revenue from oil exports. Japan has the highest level of public-sector debt in the world. Both Greece and Italy are considered to have serious debt problems — more so than Japan — even though Japan's debt is higher. Japan has been able to fund its debt by selling to domestic savers, while Greece and Italy have found it harder to sell debt as investors are more pessimistic about their economies.

CHANGES IN DEBT LEVELS

UK debt peaked after the First and Second World Wars. This shows that governments are able to borrow surprisingly large amounts without causing economic problems. After the Second World War, when debt was already very high, the United Kingdom established the National Health Service, nationalized many industries and built new houses. Debt rose to over 220 percent of GDP, but the 1950s and 1960s were periods of rapid economic growth and debt fell consistently for the next 40 years. It should be noted that after the Second World War, the United Kingdom was helped by a generous loan from the United States, which made high levels of debt easier to sustain.

HOW MUCH CAN A GOVERNMENT BORROW?

Those on the right of the political spectrum tend to see government borrowing as damaging to the economy.

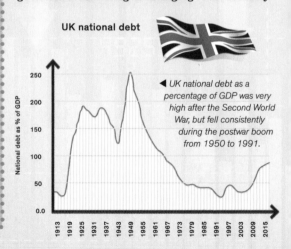

UK national debt

◀ UK national debt as a percentage of GDP was very high after the Second World War, but fell consistently during the postwar boom from 1950 to 1991.

Higher Debt

BAD

Higher debt interest payments

→

Higher taxes in future

→

Higher interest rates

NOT SO BAD

Borrowing increases demand in recession

→

Borrowing finances public investment

→

Increase in GDP, which helps increase tax revenue

▲ Higher national debt is not necessarily a bad thing — it depends on why the government is borrowing and what it is using the debt for.

They believe that high debt leads to higher interest payments (which demands the levying of higher taxes in order to make those payments) and raises the possibility of future default on debts. They also argue that government borrowing is indicative of wasteful government spending that crowds out the more efficient private sector (see Crowding Out, page 224). Finally, higher debt levels lead to an increased burden on future generations.

However, other economists argue that government borrowing can be necessary — for example, in a recession, rising debt helps to offset the fall in private spending. Also, debt can enable the government to invest in education, health care and infrastructure, which help to boost long-term productivity and future economic growth. The desirability of debt depends on a number of factors.

"DESIRABILITY OF DEBT"

• • • • • • • • • • • • •

Levels of domestic saving. If there is a shortage of domestic savings, it will be harder to finance the deficit.

Economic growth. If real GDP increases by 3 percent, debt-to-GDP ratio can be reduced without increasing tax rates. Suppose the national debt increases by 1 percent, and GDP rises by 3 percent — the debt-to-GDP ratio has fallen despite rising debt! The decline in U.S. and UK debt ratios in the postwar period came about because of a prolonged period of economic growth. The real problem occurs when high levels of debt occur alongside economic stagnation.

Foreign ownership. If a country relies on foreign investors to buy bonds, it makes the debt more vulnerable to capital flight. For example, if UK debt is owned by foreign investors, a fall in the value of the pound could make investors sell and the debt would be harder to finance.

Trust. In Japan, debt is 227.9 percent of GDP, but bond yields are very low because domestic investors still trust the Japanese government. In other countries there is greater pessimism about the long-term fortunes of the economy. In Greece, where the government struggles to collect tax revenue, and is faced with a declining economy, the prospect of debt default is relatively high.

ECONOMIC GROWTH

GDP is a measure of national output and national income, and economic growth means there is an increase in real GDP. In theory, economic growth increases living standards as average incomes rise and individuals are able to enjoy more goods and services.

THE IMPORTANCE OF ECONOMIC GROWTH

Just 150 years ago, living standards in the Western world were unrecognizable from those we know today, with many workers struggling to make ends meet. Poverty was widespread and life expectancy much lower. Economic growth has been important for improving living standards, reducing poverty and enabling a more diversified economy. Economic growth also enables more to be spent on public services such as education, health care and environmental services. Moreover, economic growth should allow a higher percentage of time to be devoted to leisure activities.

The length of the working day has fallen since the 19th century, but the utopian vision of Keynes' 15-hour working week has not been realized yet (see work–life balance, page 96).

After the Second World War, the German and Japanese economies were devastated. However, they managed to rebuild and create economic growth. This growth enabled them to reinvest the proceeds in improving productive capacity, causing further economic growth.

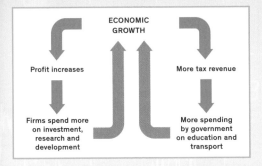

▲ *The virtuous cycle of economic growth. Higher growth enables more investment, leading to improved long-term growth.*

CAUSES OF ECONOMIC GROWTH

In the long term, the most important determinant of economic growth is technological innovation. In the preindustrial age, a large workforce was needed to manually cultivate food. In the modern age, new technology can enable a much smaller workforce to produce sufficient food. Workers can leave the fields and move to the cities to work in factories. The lower costs of food production also mean a smaller percentage of income goes toward food, leaving more to be spent on other goods.

In 1800, most people of working age were involved in agriculture. By 1900, new technology meant the same quantity of food could be produced with fewer workers, enabling people to move to factories and produce more manufactured goods.

By 2000, new technology had also improved labor productivity in factories, enabling workers to move to the service sector (e.g., retail, cleaning and health).

The important factor in economic growth is new technology, which enables higher labor productivity. This means that, even if the population stays the same, more goods can be produced by the same number of workers.

In recent decades, it is the widespread use of computers and the development of the Internet that have further increased people's productivity.

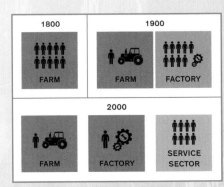

▲ *In 1800, most people worked on farms. In 1900, improved technology enabled people to leave the land and work in factories. This improved productivity and was vital for economic growth.*

CHINESE ECONOMIC MIRACLE

Between 1985 and 2015, China had the fastest-growing economy in the world, with an average annual growth rate of approximately 10 percent. Average growth rates in the United States and Europe were closer to 2 percent. What caused this very high growth in China?

STEPS TO GROWTH

The old communist-style economy was very inefficient. State-owned companies had few incentives. As the economy was liberalized, companies had very large potential efficiency savings. China was able to "catch up" with more developed economies:

- Inefficient state-owned industries are privatized.
- Price controls are liberalized.
- The country is opened up to foreign investment and free trade.

- Stock markets are opened and the banking sector is developed (1990).
- Low wages and low prices drive Chinese manufacturing exports.
- Growth in exporting industries brings economies of scale.
- Growth and profit enable more investment and capital accumulation.

Another factor that helped Chinese manufacturing growth was a plentiful supply of cheap labor. In the early 1980s, a high percentage of the Chinese workforce worked on small farms for very low wages. As industry expanded in the southeast of the country, there was an elastic supply of labor willing to work for relatively low wages (but still higher than those paid by agriculture). This helped China to gain a comparative advantage in labor-intensive manufacturing — Chinese companies were able to undercut their Western rivals, which had much higher labor costs.

China's strong economic growth has created a virtuous cycle, with high growth and increasing profits leading to rising real incomes, growing demand and also greater capital accumulation, which enables more investment.

ECONOMIC CYCLE

The economic cycle is not always steady, and an economy will inevitably experience peaks and troughs. If policymakers are not careful, this may lead to so-called boom and bust.

ECONOMIC BOOM

In a period of rising wages and rising house prices, consumers will feel more confident and increase their spending. The rise in demand will drive economic growth and encourage companies to invest and expand production. This investment creates more jobs and demand, leading to higher economic growth.

BOOM AND BUST

However, it is possible to have too much of a good thing. If demand rises rapidly, companies may be unable to keep pace.

If companies can't increase supply in the short term, they will respond by putting up prices to maximize revenue and reduce demand. This leads to inflation and is a sign that the economy is overheating. To reduce inflation, a central bank may decide to increase interest rates, which will reduce demand.

In a boom, consumers may also get carried away and increase spending by borrowing on credit cards. This happened just before the Wall Street Crash of 1929 — when people borrowed to buy shares and cars. When interest rates rise to reduce inflation, consumers with significant debt are suddenly much worse off and have to reduce their spending.

From a period of high growth, the economy

can quickly change. As confidence falls, people cut back on spending and try to pay off their debts. This can result in falling demand, leading to lower output and lower investment and a further drop in demand. And this can cause a recession, as GDP falls and unemployment rises. In response, companies will cut back on investment, which also reduces growth. Eventually, this period of bust will end as consumers begin to spend again, taking us back to the start of the economic cycle.

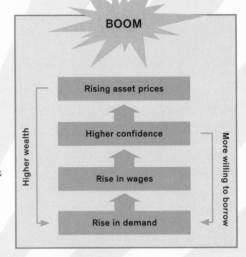

BOOM

Higher wealth

Rising asset prices

↑

Higher confidence

↑

Rise in wages

↑

Rise in demand

More willing to borrow

▲ Factors that can cause an economic boom.

SECULAR STAGNATION

Secular stagnation describes a general slowdown in rates of economic growth and an end to the cycle of boom and bust. Since the financial crisis of 2008, economic growth rates have fallen well below average postwar growth rates.

What has caused this secular stagnation? **Weakness of global demand.** Problems both in the Eurozone and globally affect overall demand.

Low wage growth. Globalization and new technology have played a role in keeping wage growth lower. A greater share of GDP has been diverted to retained profit rather than wage growth, limiting demand in the economy.

Market glut. An excess supply in many markets, including steel, cars and oil, has caused many companies to struggle.

Globalization. The competitiveness of the world economy is increasing, putting downward pressure on prices.

Inflation targeting by central banks. This has helped to avoid cycles of boom and bust, which were more common in the 1970s and 1980s. Inflation rates have been falling across the developed world. Once, this would have been seen as a good thing, but as we get closer to deflation, the fear is that this will depress normal growth.

STRUCTURAL FACTORS

Secular stagnation is partly related to limited demand, but some economists point to long-term structural factors. Many Western economies have a rapidly aging population, which reduces the size of the working population and increases the old-age dependency ratio (see page 90). And although we live, in the West, in a high-tech society, many argue that improvements in technology are becoming more marginal compared to past technological leaps, and there are diminishing returns on productivity increases. It can become harder to increase productivity in the increasingly important service sector, which is labor intensive. Furthermore, environmental problems could increase pressure on limited commodities. If these factors are permanent, we could be looking at lower rates of economic growth in the future.

LOW GROWTH

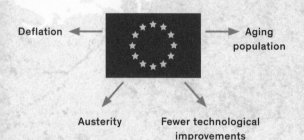

Deflation ← ★ ★ ★ ★ ★ → Aging population

↓ Austerity   ↓ Fewer technological improvements

◀ *It is feared that the global economy, and the Eurozone in particular, faces a period of secular stagnation. Europe has an aging population and has experienced fiscal austerity, periods of deflation/low growth, and high unemployment.*

ARE WE TOO PESSIMISTIC?

There have been many occasions where people have underestimated the potential for new technology. Back in the early 19th century, the British cleric and student of political economy and demography Thomas Malthus (1766–1834) predicted that a rising population would soon outstrip potential food production, causing famine, many deaths and a return to subsistence farming. (No wonder economics was labeled the dismal science!) Malthus' predictions of imminent disaster have failed to come to pass. Perhaps in a decade we will look back at the 2010s as an unusually difficult decade of low growth.

◀ *Thomas Malthus wrote "An Essay on the Principle of Population" (1798). He argued that the population was likely to grow faster than our ability to feed it.*

RECESSION

A recession means we are experiencing negative economic growth — in other words, the economy is becoming smaller.

WHAT HAPPENS IN A RECESSION?

Unemployment rises. Firms sell fewer goods and cut back on recruitment. In deep recessions, companies will increasingly go out of business, causing job losses.

Government borrowing increases. Job losses mean that income tax revenue falls, but governments are committed to spending more on unemployment benefits.

Consumers cut back. Spending is reduced and there is a rise in saving rates.

Inflation falls. To try to sell surplus stock, companies cut the price of goods.

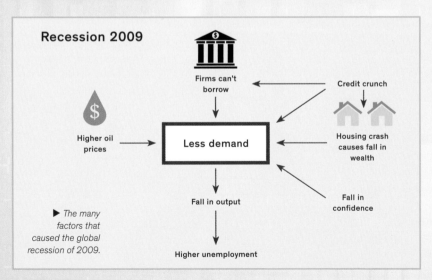

Recession 2009

Firms can't borrow

Credit crunch

Higher oil prices

Less demand

Housing crash causes fall in wealth

Fall in output

Fall in confidence

Higher unemployment

▶ The many factors that caused the global recession of 2009.

WHAT CAUSES RECESSIONS?

Most recessions are caused by a demand-side shock. This is an event that causes a fall in consumer spending or investment. In 2008–09 the global economy was affected by the financial crisis, which led to a fall in bank lending and a decline in consumer confidence. The recession was worsened by the fall in house prices and rise in oil prices.

In the United States in 1980–82, high inflation caused the Federal Reserve to increase interest rates. This rise in interest rates depressed demand and led to a recession.

SUPPLY-SIDE SHOCKS

Recessions can also be caused by a supply-side shock. This is usually a rapid rise in oil prices that increases costs and depresses demand. The most notable supply-side recession was that of 1973–74, caused by OPEC quadrupling oil prices. This resulted in a rise in prices and a decline in disposable income. It also contributed to the 1973–74 stock market crash, which further eroded investor confidence. The cost-push inflation led to a period of stagflation — falling output and rising prices.

In 2008, just as the financial crisis was hitting demand, a rapid rise in oil prices led to the double whammy of reduced bank lending and reduced consumer spending.

REAL BUSINESS CYCLE

The real business cycle theory argues that recessions are caused by supply-side factors such as changes in technology and productivity. The theory suggests that recessions are a natural and inevitable feature of modern economies and are not caused by market failure and a lack of demand.

The implication is that governments cannot prevent recessions and government intervention will only make them worse — so, for example,

an expansionary fiscal policy will lead to higher and more inefficient government spending, inflation and increased debt.

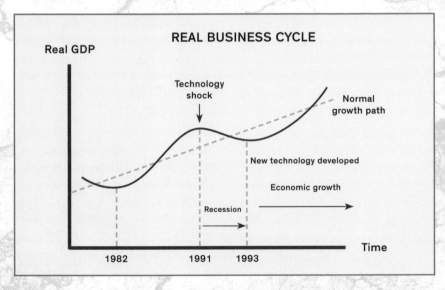

▲ *When economic growth deviates from the normal path, this is due to external shocks such as new technology.*

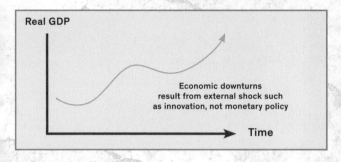

Real GDP

Economic downturns
result from external shock such
as innovation, not monetary policy

Time

◀ *Fluctuations
in a real business
cycle are caused by
external shocks.*

CAN RECESSIONS BE BENEFICIAL?

Some analysts even go so far as to say that recessions are beneficial. U.S. President Herbert Hoover famously reported that Secretary of the Treasury Andrew Mellon had advised him during the Great Depression to: "liquidate labor, liquidate stocks, liquidate farmers, liquidate real estate ... it will purge the rottenness out of the system ... people will work harder, live a more moral life."

The argument is that inefficient companies go out of business in a recession, and there are greater incentives for surviving companies to cut costs and become more efficient. In the long run the economy benefits from this purge of inefficiency, and some famous companies, such as General Motors and Disney, were founded during a deep recession.

However, other economists argue that this ignores strong empirical evidence showing that recessions can last a long time and are caused by a drop in private-sector spending. And it is very controversial to argue that recessions are "beneficial," when they often cause long-term economic damage:

- Unemployment is one of the biggest causes of poverty, mental illness, depression and stress. Even short-term unemployment can be very difficult for those affected.
- If there is a rise in unemployment, those who are made redundant may find it more difficult to get back into work in the future — a hysteresis effect (see page 152).
- Some good, efficient companies may go out of business because of a temporary lack of demand and the inability to borrow sufficient funds.
- Investment will fall sharply in a recession, causing lower productive capacity in the future. Since the 2008–2009 recession, many economies in Europe have failed to return to their former rates of economic growth.

BALANCE OF PAYMENTS

The balance of payments is a measure of a country's transactions with the rest of the world. It is concerned with imports and exports and financial flows.

There are two main components of the balance of payments:

- Current account: this records the value of imports and exports of goods (the trade balance), services and investment incomes and current transfers.
- Financial/capital account: this records capital flows — for example, savings deposits that are moved from one country to another, or a foreign company building a factory in another country.

If a country has a current account deficit it finances the deficit by attracting capital flows. In other words, a deficit on the current account requires a surplus on the financial/capital account.

The United States has a current account deficit, importing more goods from China and Japan than it exports. China and Japan gain United States dollars from their exports, and they use this foreign currency to invest in the United States. A Japanese firm may build a factory and manufacture cars in the U.S. itself, while China uses its foreign currency earnings to buy U.S. assets, such as U.S. government bonds. These capital flows from China and Japan. enable the United States to gain back the dollars it has spent on imports, which in turn enables it to import more goods.

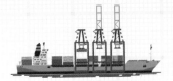

China's large current account surplus is mirrored by deficits in countries like the United States and the United Kingdom. In other words, the current account deficit is financed by a surplus on the financial/capital account.

WHAT WOULD HAPPEN IF CHINA STOPPED BUYING U.S. ASSETS?

Suppose China decided to stop buying U.S. assets, and instead bought euro assets or kept money in China. With less demand for U.S. assets, there would be a fall in demand for the U.S. dollar. This fall in demand for the dollar would cause a depreciation in the dollar compared to the Chinese yuan. This would make U.S. exports relatively more competitive and it would increase the price of imports from China. As a result, U.S. consumers would buy fewer Chinese goods and more U.S.-produced goods. This would reduce the U.S. current account deficit.

In other words, as long as there are flexible exchange rates, the balance of payments is in theory self-correcting. The U.S. current account deficit requires these capital flows from China and Japan. If the capital flows dried up, the dollar would devalue and the current account deficit would reduce.

BALANCE OF PAYMENTS EQUILIBRIUM

• • • • •

• In a floating exchange rate, a deficit on the current account will be matched by a surplus on the financial/capital account and vice versa.

• If there is an increase in interest rates in one country, this would cause inflows of saving and a surplus on the financial account.

• However, inflows of money would also cause an appreciation in the exchange rate. This makes exports less competitive and imports cheaper, leading to a deficit on the current account.

• There is a self-correcting mechanism in the balance of payments.

WHY DOES CHINA KEEP BUYING U.S. ASSETS?

• • • • • • • • • • •

Why is China keen to buy U.S. assets and indirectly help the U.S. government and U.S. companies finance their debts? One reason is that China has a vested interest in keeping the dollar relatively strong and the yuan relatively weak. By buying U.S. assets, China keeps its currency weaker and its exports more competitive. This leads to higher growth in China, arguably at the expense of U.S. economic growth. (It should be noted that the yuan has appreciated in recent years.) Furthermore, purchasing U.S. assets is a good way of building up foreign currency reserves, which can be sold in a crisis.

▼ In 2008, China and Japan had a large current account surplus. This was mirrored by current account deficit in the United States. and United Kingdom. After the global recession of 2008–2009, China's surplus declined as the United States bought relatively fewer imports.

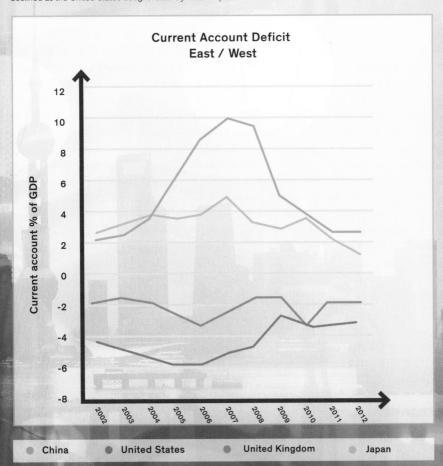

CURRENT ACCOUNT DEFICIT

A current account deficit essentially means that the value of imports is greater than the value of exports. (Strictly, net investment income and current transfers must also be taken into account.)

At first glance, a current account deficit is a bad thing, implying that we are living beyond our means. In 2003, legendary U.S. investor Warren Buffett said of the United States:

In effect, our country has been behaving like an extraordinarily rich family that possesses an immense farm. In order to consume 4 percent more than we produce — that's the trade deficit — we have, day by day, been both selling pieces of the farm and increasing the mortgage on what we still own."

Warren Buffett

However, as with so many economic issues, the importance of a current account deficit depends on many factors. A deficit isn't necessarily a bad thing.

CURRENT ACCOUNT DEFICIT IN THE 19TH CENTURY

During the second half of the 19th century, the United States ran a persistent current account deficit, but during this period attracted significant capital inflows. For example, British investors helped to finance the building of the new U.S. railway network. These capital flows helped both to increase the productive capacity of the U.S. economy and to finance the U.S. current account deficit. The investment in the railways proved profitable and rail companies gained

increased income to pay the interest on the loans from the United Kingdom.

This period of current account deficit and inward investment helped to make the U.S. economy the strongest in the world — demonstrating that a current account deficit is consistent with a strengthening economy. After the First World War, U.S. industry was in a very strong position, and the United States was able to become the world's leading exporter — for many years it ran a current account surplus, leading to a buildup of foreign assets owned by U.S. companies.

CURRENT ACCOUNT DEFICIT AFTER 1982

Since 1982 the U.S. economy has experienced a persistent current account deficit, peaking at close to 7 percent of GDP in 2006. The U.S. current account deficit has been caused by several factors.

Decline in domestic savings. Consumers are spending a higher percentage of income rather than saving. This has led to relatively higher consumption of imports.

Emergence of new exporters. China and Southeast Asia have been more competitive compared to the United States.

United States seen as safe haven for portfolio investment. This has led to sustained demand for U.S. bonds and U.S. assets, the resulting capital flows helping to finance and sustain the large current account deficit.

Strength of dollar. Because of the demand for U.S. assets, the dollar has remained strong despite the current account deficit. A strong dollar makes U.S. exports more expensive and imports cheaper.

The U.S. current account deficit has shrunk from 6 percent of GDP in 2006 to 2.5 percent of GDP in 2015 (helped by improved energy production and a decline in imports). It shows that the U.S. deficit of 6 percent was perhaps not as serious as Buffett feared.

BALANCE OF PAYMENTS CRISIS

A balance of payments crisis occurs when a country cannot buy essential imports or pay the interest on its debt, or both. It generally leads to a rapid and destabilizing depreciation in the currency, and is more common in emerging economies.

HOW A BALANCE OF PAYMENTS CRISIS CAN OCCUR

An emerging economy attracts loans from abroad to finance investment and consumption. This leads to higher economic growth and encourages banks in the developed world to lend more money, which can be used to pay the interest on current loans and finance more investment and spending.

But suppose some external event causes investors to lose confidence in the emerging economy. For example, the emerging economy relies on oil exports and is hit by a fall in oil prices. The loss in confidence brings the inward flow of foreign currency to an end. Falling growth means the emerging economy struggles to meet interest repayments, and foreign investors become nervous and try to remove their foreign investment or demand higher interest rates (or both). Because of falling growth and high interest rates, the emerging economy must spend a high percentage of its income on interest repayments, leading to a shortage of currency with which to buy essential imports. The currency of the emerging economy starts to fall rapidly in value because people no longer want to buy it, preferring safer assets like the dollar. The rapid fall in the currency makes imports more expensive and discourages investment.

External shock:
fall in oil prices

Loss of confidence

Capital flight
"save abroad"

Currency falls
further

High foreign debt

Currency falls

Inflation

Balance of
payments crisis

◀ *For a country that relies on oil production, a fall in oil prices can cause a balance of payments crisis. With less income, it is harder to pay foreign debt, and the currency falls, leading to inflation. All this promotes a loss of confidence, which causes the currency to fall further.*

1. Buildup of foreign debt.

2. External shock causes fall in economic growth and less income to pay off foreign debt.

3. Currency falls. This makes it harder to pay foreign debt.

4. Currency falls — people lose confidence in the economy. Investors seek a safer haven.

It also makes it harder to repay loans denominated in foreign currency. To try to stop the fall in the currency, the emerging economy decides to put up interest rates to attract saving, but this leads to lower economic growth and a negative cycle of falling output.

ESCAPING A BALANCE OF PAYMENTS CRISIS

Balance of payments crises are not permanent. First, the country may receive emergency funds from abroad, for example, a loan from IMF to help stabilize the economy. Second, the fall in the exchange rate can make a country's exports more competitive; over time it can benefit from increasing exports. Also, the country may place limits on capital withdrawal. This can slow down the exodus of capital from the economy.

EXCHANGE RATES

The exchange rate reflects the value at which one currency can be traded against another. For example, in September 2016 the exchange rate between the U.S. dollar and the pound sterling was $1 = £0.75, or £1 = $1.33.

WHAT DETERMINES MOVEMENTS IN THE EXCHANGE RATE?

Inflation and exchange rates. Exchange rates are determined by supply and demand factors, and are closely related to the fortunes of the respective economies. Over the long term, relative inflation rates are important. If inflation in the United States was permanently higher than that of its main competitors, U.S. goods would become less competitive and we would see a fall in demand for U.S. goods and a rise in U.S. demand for imports. This would lead to a depreciation in the U.S. dollar.

After the Second World War, the strongest currencies were the German deutsche mark and Japanese yen because, for the most part, those countries' economies had low inflation, rising productivity and successful export sectors.

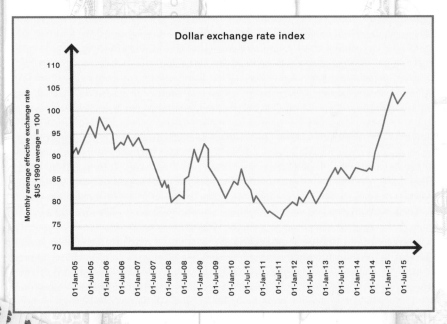

Dollar exchange rate index

Monthly average effective exchange rate $US 1990 average = 100

▲ The effective exchange rate looks at the value of the dollar against a weighted basket of currencies. It gives the overall performance of the dollar. From this graph we can see that the dollar appreciated by approximately 35 percent between 2011 and 2015.

VALUE OF THE DOLLAR

Higher economic growth. Over the period of 2012 to 2015, the United States was recovering from the global financial crisis at a quicker rate than the Eurozone. The higher economic growth encouraged more confidence in the U.S. economy and increased the prospect of higher U.S. interest rates. This attracted foreign investment.

Current account deficit. A current account deficit means the value of imports and other money outflows is greater than the value of exports and other money inflows; in other words, currency is leaving the country. This tends to cause a fall in the value of the currency. From 2011 to 2014, the U.S. current account deficit fell from 3.2 percent of GDP to 2.2 percent of GDP due to stronger exports and a relative decline in energy imports. This increased demand for the dollar.

Safe haven. In troubled times, investors prefer the "security" of U.S. assets compared to the instability of troubled or emerging economies. The dollar appreciated after 2009 because global investors saw it as a relative safe haven compared to other currencies, such as the sinking euro.

Speculation. Trillions of dollars are traded on global currency markets as investors seek to profit from predicting exchange rate movements. As a result, exchange rate movements often reflect little more than the changing sentiments of market traders.

When the United Kingdom voted to leave the European Union in June 2016, the pound fell 15 percent in value within a few weeks because investors predicted that, once the United Kingdom was outside the European Union's single market, there would be less demand to invest and save in the UK economy.

GOLD STANDARD

The gold standard (see page 241) was an attempt to fix the value of currencies directly against the value of gold. The gold standard aimed to keep inflation low and provide stable exchange rates to promote international trade.

However, economist John Maynard Keynes criticized the gold standard for deflationary pressures and for possibly creating uncompetitive exchange rates.

In the Great Depression, it was felt the gold standard contributed to deflation and recession. Countries started to leave the gold standard in order to devalue their currency, making exports more competitive. The gold standard has not been revived.

IMPORTANCE OF INTEREST RATES

• • • • • • • • •

Suppose you are an investment bank and want to get the best rate of interest on your savings. The interest rate in both Europe and the United States is 0.5 percent. If interest rates are the same, it doesn't matter whether you invest in the United States or in Europe. But if U.S. interest rates go up to 1.5 percent, it is worth moving millions of euros of savings to the United States because you will get a better rate of return. Therefore, investors will sell euros and buy dollars. This causes an appreciation in the value of the dollar. Even the prospect of higher interest rates is enough for investors to buy dollars in anticipation of a rise in value.

In truth, the gold standard is already a barbarous relic.
John Maynard Keynes

DEVALUATION

If a currency experiences a large devaluation or depreciation, is this good or bad for the economy?

The devaluation of a currency makes exports cheaper, but imports will be more expensive. Suppose the pound-to-dollar exchange rate is £1 = $1.50. If someone in the United Kingdom wants to buy a $3 apple pie, it will cost them £2. If the pound is devalued, and the exchange rate is now £1 = $1.20, the same $3 apple pie will cost the UK consumer £2.50.

Meanwhile, in the United States, a £10,000 British-made car is listed for $15,000, but after the pound is devalued, the same car is just $12,000. The result is that the United Kingdom will export more cars and import fewer apple pies.

The big winners will be exporters in the country that has devalued its currency, who will see a rise in demand for their relatively cheaper goods. Overall, that economy should see a rise in domestic demand and economic growth, because there is more demand for exports and less demand for imports. A devaluation should also reduce the current account deficit, because exports rise relative to imports (depending on the elasticity of demand). If demand is inelastic, a devaluation will lead to only a small increase in quantity of exports. If demand is elastic, there will be a bigger percentage increase in demand.

The big losers will be those economies that import goods from abroad to sell domestically. Goods will be more expensive and consumers will see a relative decline in purchasing power. Currency devaluation also tends to cause inflation. This is because:

- Imports are more expensive.
- Rising domestic demand causes demand-pull inflation, to wit, "too much money chasing too few goods."

- Exporters have less incentive to cut costs (because they are more competitive without making any effort).

SOME DEVALUATIONS CAN BE VERY BENEFICIAL

If a country is in recession, then a devaluation will help to boost domestic demand.

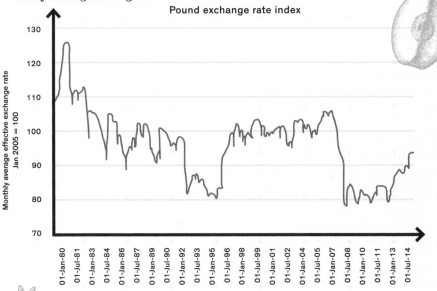

Pound exchange rate index

▲ This graph shows the value of the pound sterling. It highlights two big falls — the devaluation of 1992 and the depreciation of 2008 due to the financial crisis.

In 1992, the United Kingdom was in the European Exchange Rate Mechanism (ERM). It was trying to keep the value of the pound high, which meant maintaining high interest rates. However, an overvalued currency and high interest rates caused a recession.

On Wednesday September 16, 1992, the British Government was forced to withdraw the pound from the ERM because it couldn't maintain its value. As a result it depreciated 20 percent. Seen at the time as a catastrophe, it became known as "Black Wednesday." But this depreciation led to cheaper exports and uncompetitive imports and also lower interest rates, which led to a strong economic recovery. Because of spare capacity in the economy, inflation was muted and unemployment fell.

POSITIVES AND NEGATIVES OF DEVALUATION

POSITIVES
- Good for companies that export abroad
- Foreign holidays are cheaper
- Economic growth tends to rise
- Jobs are more secure

NEGATIVES
- Bad for consumers who buy expensive imports
- Bad for companies that import raw materials
- Inflation tends to increase

Russian central bank raised interest rates to 13–17 percent, but struggled to stem the decline in the value of the ruble, while inflation rose to 11 percent. The hope is that the devaluation will help rebalance the Russian economy, with a move away from oil production to manufacturing exports. But this rebalancing can be difficult to achieve.

INTERNAL DEVALUATION

In a fixed exchange rate, a country can't devalue its currency. To regain competitiveness, the alternative is to reduce wages, prices and costs. This is known as internal devaluation because you try to achieve the same effect without changing the value of your currency. However, reducing prices, wages and costs can be much harder work because workers tend to resist wage cuts. Devaluation of currency is much easier!

HARMFUL DEVALUATIONS

The 1992 devaluation was beneficial for the UK economy, but it doesn't mean devaluations are always beneficial. In 2011, Belarus devalued the Belarusian ruble by 62 percent over the course of the year, but this led to inflation of 108 percent and interest rates of 45 percent. This kind of devaluation is very destabilizing — people seek to hold funds in other currencies, and the devaluation and inflation discourage investment.

In 2014, Russia started to see a similar depreciation in the ruble when its economy suffered because of collapsing oil prices. In response, the

PURCHASING POWER PARITY

The purchasing power of a currency refers to how much of a currency is needed to purchase a typical basket of goods. Purchasing power parity gives the effective exchange rate that would be able to buy the same quantity of goods and services with, for example, either dollars or pounds. Suppose a pint of beer costs £3 in the United Kingdom and $2 in the United States — purchasing power parity is therefore £1 = $1.50.

UK — £3.00

U.S. — $2.00

Purchasing power parity £1 = $1.50

THE LAW OF ONE PRICE

The concept of purchasing power parity derives from the law of one price, which states that, in the absence of transaction costs and trade barriers, goods should sell for the same price when expressed in the same currency. If goods were cheaper in Canada, U.S. consumers could drive there to buy — pushing up Canadian prices and putting downward pressure on U.S. prices.

THE BIG MAC INDEX

SIX MOST EXPENSIVE
(NOVEMBER 15, 2015)
1. Switzerland: $6.82 (6.50 CHF)
2. Norway: $5.65 (46 NOK)
3. Sweden: $5.13 (43.70 SEK)
4. Denmark: $5.08 (34.59 DKK)
5. United States: $4.79 (USD)
6. Israel: $4.63 (18.05 ILS)

SIX CHEAPEST (JULY 2015)
1. Venezuela: $0.67 (4.22 VEF)
2. Ukraine: $1.55 (15.74 UAH)
3. India: $1.83 (121.21 INR)
4. Russia: $1.88 (133.75 RUB)
5. Malaysia: $2.01 (8.63 MYR)
6. South Africa: $2.09 (31.48 ZAR)

The Big Mac index shows the price of a Big Mac in dollars. In theory, the ingredients of a Big Mac are the same the world over, so the index shows whether exchange rates differ from purchasing power parity. In 2015, the price of a Big Mac was.

- $4.79 in the United States,
- $2.09 in South Africa (31.48 ZAR),
- $0.67 in Venezuela (4.22 VEF).

This means that $10 will buy you nearly five Big Macs in South Africa, but only two in the United States. In other words, one dollar goes further in South Africa than in the United States. Therefore, official exchange rates do not reflect the actual purchasing power parity between the United States and South Africa. In this case, the South African rand (ZAR) is 56 percent undervalued compared to the U.S. dollar.

Of course, the Big Mac is based on only one good, and *The Economist* magazine used it light-heartedly when it created the Big Mac Index in an attempt demystify real exchange rates. To get a more accurate understanding of exchange rates, you need to look at the prices in a basket of goods.

LABOR COSTS AND PURCHASING POWER

• • • • • • • • • •

The Big Mac index suggests that the cost of living in South Africa is cheaper than in the United States. However, if wages are higher in the United States, it will be relatively easy to earn enough to afford a Big Mac. If wages are much lower in South Africa, buying a Big Mac or five will take more hours of work.

WHY DO CURRENCY VALUES VARY FROM PURCHASING POWER PARITY?

One reason is instability. Investors may be more nervous about investing in South Africa because of a more uncertain political and economic climate, while the United States may be seen as more secure. And there are different living costs — in the United States, wages and business rents are generally higher, and a Big Mac needs, therefore, to be priced higher to cover the higher costs.

CHAPTER 7

ECONOMIC POLICY

MONETARY POLICY

Monetary policy is concerned with trying to target low inflation and steady economic growth. The primary tool of monetary policy is interest rates. If an economy is growing too quickly and inflation is predicted to rise, the central bank will tend to increase interest rates. So what happens when interest rates increase?

Higher interest rates increase the cost of borrowing. Companies put off investment decisions as a result and consumers spend less. Homeowners with large variable-rate mortgages will have less disposable income because

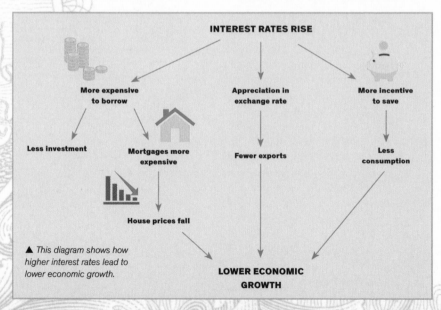

INTEREST RATES RISE

More expensive to borrow

Less investment

Mortgages more expensive

House prices fall

Appreciation in exchange rate

Fewer exports

More incentive to save

Less consumption

LOWER ECONOMIC GROWTH

▲ This diagram shows how higher interest rates lead to lower economic growth.

their monthly mortgage interest payments will increase. Higher interest rates can cause house prices to fall.

HOW INTEREST RATES EFFECT SPENDING

Suppose a homeowner has a monthly income of $2,000 and a monthly mortgage payment of $400, which leaves $1,600 to spend elsewhere. If interest rates go up from 4 percent to 6 percent, and the homeowner's monthly repayment follows suit, rising to $600, that leaves $1,400.

In 2005 and 2006, a moderate rise in interest rates had a big impact on the U.S. economy. Over the previous years, many people had taken out large mortgages that became unaffordable when interest rates rose, and there was a rise in home repossessions and a decline in house prices. This was a cause of the ensuing recession.

Higher interest rates also attract "hot money flows" (see Glossary), causing an appreciation in the currency. This appreciation makes exports less competitive, leading to lower domestic demand. Consumers also substitute some domestic consumption with consumption of imports that are more price competitive.

In summary, if the economy is overheating (growing too fast), higher interest rates are a way to put a brake on the economy, reduce the growth of

▲ William McChesney Martin was Chairman of the U.S. Federal Reserve Bank for almost 20 years.

spending and investment and prevent inflation — or as William McChesney Martin, the Chairman of the U.S. Federal Reserve Bank from 1951 to 1970, said: "Take away the punch bowl just when the party gets going."

On the other hand, lower interest rates can be a way to try to encourage investment and spending in a recession.

LOW INTEREST RATES — GOOD NEWS AND BAD NEWS

Between 2009 and 2016, much of Europe and the United States experienced very low interest rates of 0.5 percent or less.

GOOD NEWS
- Good for homeowners with mortgages.
- Good for businesses with debts.
- Government borrowing is cheaper.

BAD NEWS
- Savers get low returns.
- Borrowers can't get credit (low interest rates have made lending unprofitable for banks).

Low interest rates are good news for existing borrowers and bad news for those who have retired and are living on their savings.

It is cheaper to borrow and invest when interest rates are low, and those with personal debt will more disposable income. In theory, this should increase the rate of economic growth.

DOES MONETARY POLICY WORK?

In 2008–2009, there was a deep recession in the United States and Europe. In response, interest rates were cut from around 5 percent to a record low 0.5 percent. In theory, this cut in interest rates should have provided a boost to economic growth, reduced unemployment and helped the economy recover. However, the cut had only a minimal impact on promoting economic growth.

WHY DO LOWER INTEREST RATES SOMETIMES NOT WORK?

Banking crisis. The recession of 2008–2009 was triggered by a credit crisis that left banks very short of funds. After interest rates were cut, it was very cheap to borrow, but cheap borrowing costs are not much use when banks are not able or willing to lend. As a result, the cut in interest rates didn't help businesses to get loans.

Low confidence. As a consumer, there are many factors influencing whether you borrow to buy a luxury car. If interest rates are low, the cost of borrowing falls and that will encourage you to borrow. But in a deep recession, with banks

failing and unemployment rising, most consumers would not want to take the risk — even if interest rates are low. The recession in fact saw a rise in saving rates as people tried to pay off debts, not take on more.

Global Recession. In 2009, there was a worldwide decline in exports. It wasn't just a fall in domestic demand, but also a fall in demand from abroad. In 2009, the United Kingdom had lower interest rates and a 25 percent depreciation of the pound — but neither was enough to overcome the recession in the short term.

Fiscal austerity. In Europe, problems in the Eurozone caused rising bond yields and attempts to reduce budget deficits through "austerity" programs. Therefore, although interest rates were cut in an attempt to boost demand, government spending fell, depressing demand.

In short, if the economy and financial sector are very weak, there is no guarantee lower interest rates will boost demand and economic growth.

QUANTITATIVE EASING

Until 2009, few people had heard of quantitative easing. It certainly wasn't in many economics textbooks. But in 2009 the nature of the economic crisis caused central banks to consider "unconventional" policies. Quantitative easing seemed to rip up all the old certainties — in particular, the idea that you should never print money.

First, the central bank creates money. It doesn't actually print money, but electronically increases the amount of money it has. It's like having $10,000 in your bank and being able to magically change that $10,000 to $20,000. If only!

And now, with this newly created money, the central bank buys assets, notably government bonds and corporate bonds. This large-scale purchase of bonds causes the price of bonds to rise and the bond yield to fall (see Chapter 8) .

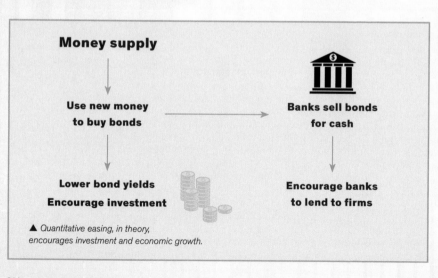

Money supply

↓

Use new money to buy bonds →

Banks sell bonds for cash

↓ ↓

**Lower bond yields
Encourage investment**

Encourage banks to lend to firms

▲ *Quantitative easing, in theory, encourages investment and economic growth.*

WHAT IS HE AIM OF QUANTITATIVE EASING?

Increase the money supply. Buying bonds from banks will increase the liquidity of banks (the amount of cash they have). The hope is that banks will be more willing to lend to businesses and consumers.

Reduce market interest rates (see Glossary). The purchase of bonds reduces the bond yield and general interest rates in the economy. The hope is that lower interest rates on corporate bonds will encourage companies to invest because borrowing is cheaper.

SO DID QUANTITATIVE EASING WORK?

The monetary base increased fourfold, but the consumer price index (CPI), which is used to measure inflation, remained very low. Overall, the success or otherwise of quantitative easing is hard to evaluate. If we want to be optimistic, we could say the recession could have been deeper and longer lasting without quantitative easing. But the effects were limited because, while the liquidity of banks increased, they remained reluctant to lend to businesses because of the poor

economic prospects. Lower interest rates didn't help significantly either — the problem was not the cost of borrowing, but the general economic climate. There is no point in companies borrowing if the prospect of future profits is gloomy.

SIDE EFFECTS OF QUANTITATIVE EASING

Governments found it easier to finance their borrowing thanks to quantitative easing. Governments usually rely on the private sector to buy bonds, but quantitative easing meant that central banks were buying bonds with created money. Lower interest rates made it much cheaper for governments, such as those of the United States and the United Kingdom, to borrow.

There were winners and losers. The biggest winners from quantitative easing were the financial institutions that were able to sell bonds and see their assets rise in value. The losers were those who relied on interest payments from bonds. Moreover, quantitative easing had a limited impact on the wider economy outside the financial markets.

What about inflation? A number of analysts predicted that quantitative easing would cause inflation, because increasing the money supply will have an effect on inflation. However, if anything, inflation has fallen during this period of quantitative easing. The increase in money supply has not led to a boom in bank lending and spending. The economy is still in a depressed state, in part because of a liquidity trap (see Glossary). In this climate, increasing the money supply has had little effect on inflation.

BETTER FORMS OF QUANTITATIVE EASING

· · · · · · · · · · · ·

Quite a few economists argue that the past forms of quantitative easing are far from perfect. Rather than buying bonds, a more effective policy would be something like a helicopter money drop that gives directly to consumers and companies (see page 218).

HELICOPTER MONEY DROP

You will almost have certainly been told as a child that "money doesn't grow on trees." But did your parents ever tell you about the economic policy to print money and drop it out of the sky?

Helicopter money involves a central bank printing money and giving it directly to private individuals. At first glance it seems to break all the laws of morality and economics, but it is held up as a solution to deflation, high unemployment and negative economic growth. It is sometimes known as "people's quantitative easing" because the new money would go to everyone, rather than just to banks that sell bonds to a central bank.

In a way, a helicopter money drop is like quantitative easing, but it leaves out the banks, which may just hoard the money anyway — if you give it to average citizens, they will spend at least some of it! The concept was popularized by Milton Friedman in his 1969 essay, "The Optimum Quantity of Money," and in recent years was taken up by Ben Bernanke, Chairman of the Federal Reserve from 2004 to 2016.

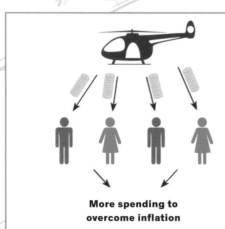

More spending to overcome inflation

◀ *A helicopter money drop involves giving money directly to ordinary people to encourage spending and economic growth.*

Suppose spending is very low because of deflation. Helicopter money would cause some higher spending and turn deflation into moderate inflation — this would help economic growth increase. If inflation overshoots, it is not so important because central banks know how to reduce inflation (e.g., increase interest rates).

the particular economic circumstances of deflation. If you print money and distribute it during normal economic circumstances, it would undoubtedly cause inflation and instability. However, it might be the most effective policy to help overcome recession if an economy is suffering from severe deflation.

I think the whole idea of the helicopter money is downright devastating. For this is nothing more than a declaration of bankruptcy of the monetary policy.

Otmar Issing, Chief Economist of the European Central Bank, 2016

WHY IS HELICOPTER MONEY CONTROVERSIAL?

Some economists fear that printing money and giving it away may cause people to lose confidence in money and that it could stoke future inflation. There is also a moral argument — the idea of printing money and giving it away seems almost hedonistic. The important thing about helicopter money is that it is appropriate only in

CASE STUDY — JAPAN

Japan has suffered from periods of deflation during the 1990s, 2000s and 2010s. The Bank of Japan has considered helicopter money as a drastic step to overcome deflationary pressures in their economy. However, despite intentions to overcome deflation, the Bank of Japan has always been reluctant to actually commit to helicopter money.

Since there are no successful examples of helicopter money drops in the real world, this approach has remained theoretical conjecture. It is easier to follow a policy when there is evidence of success elsewhere in the world. It is harder to be the first to commit to an untried policy.

FISCAL POLICY

Fiscal policy involves changing taxation and government spending levels to influence the rate of economic growth. In theory, fiscal policy can be a useful tool for overcoming recession and high unemployment. However, critics argue that it is ineffective and an excuse for higher government spending.

HOW CAN GOVERNMENT BORROWING HELP IN A RECESSION?

In a recession, we tend to see a rapid increase in saving and a complementary fall in private-sector spending and investment, leading to negative economic growth. To solve unemployment, the classical response is to reduce wages so companies can afford labor. However, if you cut wages, workers have less money, causing further falls in demand.

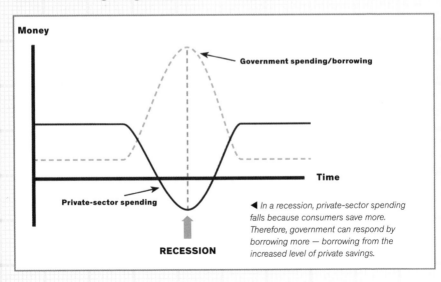

◀ In a recession, private-sector spending falls because consumers save more. Therefore, government can respond by borrowing more — borrowing from the increased level of private savings.

John Maynard Keynes argued that in a period of mass unemployment, it could take a very long time for the unused savings to become used — those savings were wasted resources. He argued that the government could speed up economic recovery by borrowing from the private sector and injecting this stagnant money into the economy.

This government spending would create jobs and increase overall spending. This would result in a positive multiplier effect and help to get the economy out of recession. Because savings rise in a recession, the government is easily able to borrow.

In other words, the rise in government debt mirrors a fall in private-sector debt.

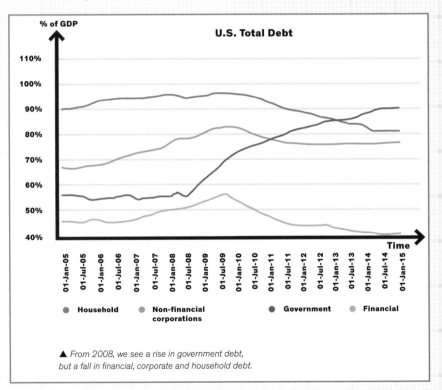

▲ *From 2008, we see a rise in government debt, but a fall in financial, corporate and household debt.*

FISCAL POLICY DURING A BOOM

When the economy is growing and unemployment is low, a government can reduce the budget deficit or even run a budget surplus. If inflation is getting out of hand, higher taxes can reduce excess spending and also lead to a budget surplus. Keynesian fiscal policy isn't necessarily about bigger government, but about the willingness to borrow in a recession to provide an economic stimulus. The Great Depression provided a convincing case study for this new economic theory — markets did not seem to self-correct, with recessions and mass unemployment persisting for several years in many Western economies.

KEYNES THE ADVOCATE

Keynes tried hard to challenge the economic orthodoxy with imaginative ideas. One anecdote has it that in a restaurant during the Great Depression, Keynes noticed that some waiters were idle and he started to throw napkins on the floor for the waiters to pick up. Keynes argued that he was trying to keep the waiters employed, and that this was the most important objective in the Great Depression.

Keynes once made a case for the government to set the unemployed to work digging holes in the ground and then filling them up. When he mentioned this, the interviewer responded, "But wouldn't it be better to employ people to build hospitals?" Keynes reply was "Excellent, build hospitals! But the point is the main task is to end the unemployment of resources. Whether you dig holes or build hospitals, it doesn't matter. As long as we employ the unemployed to do something." Keynes wanted people to suggest building hospitals so they would support the economic stimulus, but for him the key issue was to provide additional demand.

▲ The primary importance of fiscal policy is to help get the unemployed back to work during a major recession.

CRITICISM OF FISCAL POLICY

- Monetary policy is often preferred because it avoids political decisions about where to spend money or cut taxes.
- Expansionary fiscal policy can lead to inefficient government spending because it can be hard to find good schemes for billions of dollars of investment.
- Some claim that Keynesianism invariably leads to bigger government. It's easy to increase public-sector spending, but once established it becomes hard to cut.
- It is difficult to fine-tune an economy. Fiscal policy takes time to have an effect, and it is hard to know what will happen to an economy in the future.
- Some have said fiscal policy is like driving a car. But a car that only allows you to look out of a partially obscured rear window. Furthermore, when you turn the steering wheel, there is a delay as the car changes direction.

This is what fiscal policy is like — you have to guess the direction by looking at past economic data. When you try to influence aggregate demand, there could be a delay of up to a year or more, so it is easy to make the wrong decision.

▲ *John Maynard Keynes, the most influential economist of the 20th century, revolutionized economics with new theories on demand management.*

REVIVAL OF KEYNESIANISM

To a large extent, Keynesian demand management fell out of favor during the 1970s and 1980s due to a period of stagflation. However, the great recession of 2008–2009 brought renewed interest in Keynesian fiscal policy for the following reasons:

- There were high levels of government borrowing but also very low interest rates in the United States, the United Kingdom and Japan.

- Monetary policy seemed ineffective in solving the deep recession. Many economists argued that there needed to be expansionary fiscal policy too, in order for monetary policy to be effective.

CROWDING OUT

Crowding out occurs when higher government borrowing leads to higher public-sector spending, but less private-sector spending. In other words, higher government borrowing doesn't increase overall demand.

Suppose an investor is faced with a choice — to buy corporate bonds (and lend to the private sector) or to buy a government bond (and lend to the government). If the government borrows more, it effectively takes savings and investment away from the private sector. Therefore, although government investment increases, it leads to an equivalent fall in private-sector spending, and overall demand remains the same.

But critics of government spending argue that it tends to be more inefficient and wasteful. Therefore, an expansionary

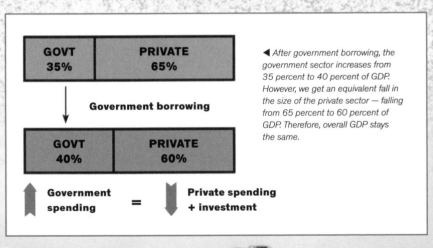

◄ *After government borrowing, the government sector increases from 35 percent to 40 percent of GDP. However, we get an equivalent fall in the size of the private sector — falling from 65 percent to 60 percent of GDP. Therefore, overall GDP stays the same.*

fiscal policy merely shifts resources from the efficient private sector to the more inefficient public sector.

HIGHER INTEREST RATES

Crowding out of the private sector may also occur due to higher interest rates, which arise from increased government borrowing. If a government needs to sell more bonds, it may have to increase bond yields in order to encourage people to buy. But a general rise in interest rates will discourage private-sector investment.

NO CROWDING OUT

However, while this crowding out may be in effect during normal economic growth, we usually see an excess of unused savings in a deep recession. When a government borrows, it uses savings that would otherwise have remained idle.

U.S. SAVING RATE

Investors don't want to risk investing in the private sector in a recession, so

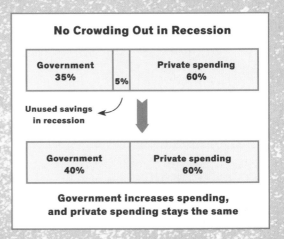

No Crowding Out in Recession

Government 35%	5%	Private spending 60%

Unused savings in recession

Government 40%	Private spending 60%

Government increases spending, and private spending stays the same

▲ *In this example, there are unused savings, so borrowing doesn't cause crowding out.*

when people buy government bonds they are not reducing private investment.

Furthermore, if a government borrows more, it doesn't necessarily cause rising interest rates. Between 2008 and 2016, we saw a large rise in the size of the U.S. national debt, but at the same time interest rates fell. This was because there was a glut of savings. In other words, higher government borrowing was compatible with lower interest rates, so there was no crowding out.

AUSTERITY

Austerity refers to policies of reducing government borrowing (by way of lower government spending and higher taxes) during a period of low growth. Austerity is particularly associated with the Eurozone's efforts to reduce government borrowing following the euro debt crisis of 2010–12.

THE SAD STORY OF GREECE

In 2008, Greek debt was already high. The economy was also struggling with uncompetitive exports and a large current account deficit. Global recession caused a further rise in debt and fall in growth. Before the crisis, Greek bond yields were very low (people thought the euro made all Eurozone debt secure). But at the start of the debt crisis, investors realized that Greece had no effective and willing lender of last resort. Bond markets feared that Greece would default on its debts and there was strong pressure to cut public spending.

In response, the Greek government pursued austerity, trying to run a primary budget surplus (see Glossary). This involved sharp cuts in government

▲ Austerity in Greece contributed to a very deep recession, mass unemployment and widespread economic suffering.

spending and higher taxes. But this austerity led to a deeper recession, as spending fell and unemployment rose to 25 percent.

Despite fiscal austerity, there was nothing to boost demand. Greek exports were uncompetitive because Greece was unable to devalue its currency. The European Central Bank (ECB) set the monetary policy for the whole Eurozone, not solely in the interests of Greece. The ECB did not want to pursue quantitative easing, so monetary policy was relatively restrictive. The deep recession also caused a further fall in tax revenues — people who are not earning do not pay any income tax. Therefore, despite austerity, government borrowing continued to rise. Furthermore, because GDP fell sharply, the debt-to-GDP ratio rose rapidly. In other words, the austerity was self-defeating — despite all the spending cuts and higher taxes, Greece saw its debt-to-GDP ratio continue to rise.

As the debt-to-GDP ratio rose, there was pressure to pursue more austerity. A lot of Greek debt was held outside Greece by European banks. It was suggested that Greece should be allowed to default on the debts it couldn't pay back. But European taxpayers and European banks were not keen on allowing Greece to default because this was considered a "reward for irresponsible borrowing," or moral hazard (see Glossary). A bailout was

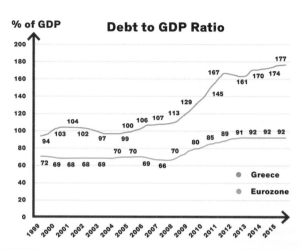

▲ Greek debt was 100 percent of GDP before the financial crisis, but by 2016 had increased to 177 percent of GDP — nearly double the average debt level in the Eurozone of 92 percent of GDP.

agreed to, but this was primarily so that Greece could pay the interest on its debts.

In the long term, a more substantial default and less austerity may have given bondholders a better return. The lesson from the Greek experience is that very deep austerity can be self-defeating; to reduce debt, it is important to prioritize economic growth, which enables higher tax revenues. A strong economy would have been better able to pay back debt.

POLITICAL APPEAL OF AUSTERITY

Keynesian demand management can have a strong economic basis, but austerity is often more politically appealing, especially if it is compared to managing household finances. As Mr Micawber put it, in Charles Dickens' *David Copperfield* (1849): "Annual income twenty pounds, annual expenditure nineteen and six, result happiness. Annual income twenty pounds, annual expenditure twenty pounds nought and six, result misery."

This sums up how many people feel about the morality of debt. Debt is seen as morally wrong in many countries, and an increase in government debt usually becomes a political liability. It is hard to explain that government debt in a recession makes use of unused savings. The overall debt burden of the economy can remain the same because the rise in private-sector saving mirrors the rise in government borrowing. While we may trust ourselves to take out a mortgage or a company to borrow for investment, there is a greater distrust that a government will borrow money and use it productively.

SUCCESSFUL REDUCTION OF THE BUDGET DEFICIT

The example of the Eurozone during the economic downturn of 2008–2009 through to 2015 suggests that there are great challenges when trying to reduce a budget deficit. But it doesn't mean reducing a budget deficit will always cause an economic downturn. It is possible to reduce levels of government borrowing and maintain high economic growth.

In the mid-1990s, Canada experienced high levels of government borrowing following its recession of 1991. By 1995 there was a budget deficit of 6 percent of GDP, and in 1995–96 a net public debt of 104 percent of GDP. This caused Canada to lose its triple-A credit rating — a serious blow for any country.

However, there was a strong political will to reduce the budget deficit. The government cut public spending and increased taxes. By 1996 the budget deficit had

fallen from 6 percent of GDP to a balanced budget; net debt fell from 104 percent of GDP to 80 percent in 1999–2000. Unlike the austerity of the Eurozone, these cuts were also achieved against the backdrop of a decade of positive economic growth and falling unemployment. Why was Canada so successful, while Greece and Spain struggled with unemployment of 25 percent?

First, Canadian interest rates were cut from 8 percent in 1995 to 3 percent in 1997. Therefore, spending cuts, which could have caused a fall in aggregate demand, could be offset by reducing interest rates to maintain demand. Second, Canada benefited from a depreciation in the Canadian dollar. In 1991 the Canadian dollar was worth US$0.89. By 1995 it stood at US$0.71, and by 1998 it had fallen to US$0.65. This fall in the value of the Canadian dollar helped to boost Canadian exports, which were also helped by a booming U.S. economy and the NAFTA agreement.

This combination of monetary easing and a fall in value of the currency helped to cushion the economy from the impact of reduced government spending. The Canadian experience shows that a government can reduce a budget deficit and public-sector spending without causing a recession or higher unemployment. But if you reduce demand from one part of the economy (the government), it is very helpful if you are able to increase demand in another (the private sector, by way of monetary policy and exports).

The problem for the Eurozone has been that macroeconomic policy is constrained by the structures of the single currency. Unlike Canada, Greece was unable to devalue its currency. Also unlike Canada, Greece could not pursue its own expansionary monetary policy.

▼ *Government spending cuts cause a fall in demand, but this can be balanced by lower interest rates and cheaper exports to maintain aggregate demand.*

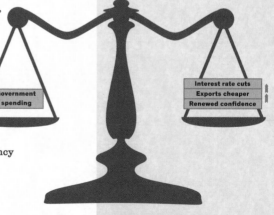

INDEPENDENT CENTRAL BANKS

Who should run the economy — unknowledgeable politicians or unelected central bankers? In recent times, most countries have delegated monetary policy to an independent central bank. This means important decisions about the economy are made by unelected experts.

ARGUMENTS FOR INDEPENDENT CENTRAL BANKS

When politicians set monetary policy we often see a politically driven business cycle. For example, the temptation is to cut interest rates in the year before an election. People feel better off, they spend more, economic growth increases and unemployment falls. The governing political party is then in a stronger position to win the election.

However, after the election, the cut in interest rate causes inflation to rise too high, and the government has to raise interest rates to reduce inflation, leading to a cycle of boom and bust. The United Kingdom used to suffer boom and bust cycles and it was one reason why the Bank of England was made independent in 1997.

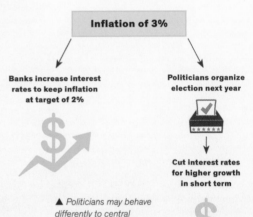

▲ Politicians may behave differently to central bankers. Politicians face temptation to cut interest rates to boost popularity.

INDEPENDENT CENTRAL BANK

The theory is that independent central bankers are not under political pressure to cut interest rates before an election. If central bankers have an inflation target, they will be willing to keep interest rates high — even if it is politically unpopular.

The Federal Reserve was given independence over U.S. monetary policy in 1913. It is criticized by those who resent its unelected powers, though it is in fact subject to oversight and scrutiny by Congress. In the relatively benign economic conditions of the 1990s and early 2000s, there was a widespread consensus that independent central banks were doing a good job. Alan Greenspan, Chairman of the Federal Reserve from 1987 to 2006, was seen in a positive light thanks to a strong economy.

> If you want a simple model for predicting the unemployment rate in the U.S. over the next few years, here it is: It will be what Greenspan wants it to be, plus or minus a random error reflecting the fact that he is not quite God.
>
> American economist Paul Krugman, 1997

CRITICISM OF CENTRAL BANKERS

However, there has been increased criticism of central bankers since the major financial crisis of 2007. The U.S. Federal Reserve was criticized for allowing a housing and credit bubble in the years leading up to 2008. Though, in defence of the Federal Reserve, there is only so much it can do with interest rates. The causes of the credit crunch were much more widespread than just interest rates being too low.

In recent years, the Federal Reserve's policy of expanding its balance sheet (increasing the monetary base) has been questioned by those who dislike "loose money." Despite its independence, the Federal Reserve cannot completely escape politics because its policies can make or break a president. You could argue that the Chairman of the Federal Reserve has more economic power than the president of the United States.

By contrast, the European central bank has been criticized for being too rigid in targeting low inflation, when during a recession there are more important economic goals, such as economic recovery and reducing unemployment.

However, despite this criticism of independent central banks and bankers, it seems unlikely that monetary policy is likely to be set by politicians in the foreseeable future. Central bankers have their limitations, but politicians perhaps have even more!

ECONOMIC FORECASTING

It is an oft-repeated joke — God created economic forecasters to make weather forecasters look good. In recent years, scientific advances have enabled weather forecasters to improve the accuracy of their predictions, but economic forecasting is still a mug's game. It is for good reason that economic forecasters are said to assume everything except responsibility! But even if economic forecasting is a tricky business, there is a need to try to predict future economic trends.

WHY IS ECONOMIC FORECASTING SO DIFFICULT?

Countless variables. We can try to model the impact of higher interest rates on consumer behavior and business investment. But nothing happens in isolation, and there are many factors affecting consumer behavior aside from higher interest rates.

Poor data. Governments produce data about key statistics, such as real GDP. However, these data are often based on incomplete statistics. For example, it takes time for companies to send income and output data to the relevant authorities, and initial data on real GDP are often later revised. If you don't know what is happening to the economy at the present time, it is hard to predict what will happen in the future. For example,

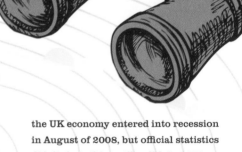

the UK economy entered into recession in August of 2008, but official statistics didn't show this until well into 2009.

Confirmation bias. Economic forecasters are subject to confirmation bias just like everyone else. If you don't like the philosophy of printing money, you are more likely to predict inflation

when a central bank increases the money supply. There are many who have been predicting inflation in the United States for many years, which has so far failed to materialize — but the predictions continue. One year, we may indeed see a return of inflation to the United States — but there is a saying: "Even a stopped clock is right twice a day."

WHY DID SO FEW ECONOMISTS PREDICT THE GLOBAL CREDIT CRUNCH AND RECESSION?

In 2000–2007 global inflation was generally low and global economic growth high. It seemed we had cracked the cycles of boom and bust of the past and achieved the holy grail of low inflationary growth and falling public-sector debt.

Many referred to this period as the great stabilization. But appearances proved deceptive.

Economists mostly ignored the impact of the financial sector and the possibility of bad loans. The credit crunch was largely unexpected because the mortgage default was on a scale that hadn't been seen before. The extent of bad loans in the system wasn't easy to spot. Economists tend to focus on headline economic statistics — inflation, economic growth, money. The number of bad loans in the banking sector wasn't so obvious because there were no headline-grabbing statistics drawing attention to them. Of course, the banks were not keen to publicize how many subprime mortgages they had on their books.

There were warning signs, such as overvalued house prices. Although even the Chairman of the Federal Reserve, Alan Greenspan, wasn't too concerned, and given his impressive track record, many people were happy to take an optimistic view.

ARE ALL ECONOMIC FORECASTS USELESS?

It would be tempting to write off all economic forecasts as useless, but that would also be a mistake. Economic forecasts can be useful, even if not foolproof.

If you try to predict economic growth and inflation in five years' time, it becomes mostly guesswork. However, it can be effective to try to model the impact of structural changes to the economy.

For example, if the Brexit negotiations for Britain to leave the European Single Market result in an increase in export tariffs of 3 percent, we can make reasonable predictions about the effect of this on exports and economic growth. However, if we try to predict how consumer confidence in the UK might be affected by Brexit, it is harder to make accurate forecasts as consumer behavior is more difficult to model.

Similarly, if a country is oil dependent, we can make useful predictions about the impact of a fall in oil prices on the economy. If you rely on oil exports and the oil price falls 50 percent, there is going to be a very clear impact on your economy. Therefore, a country that relies on oil would be wise to try to save money from oil sales and diversify the economy for the future.

HAPPINESS ECONOMICS

Happiness economics is concerned with maximizing well-being, satisfaction and general happiness, placing these goals ahead of more traditional economic targets such as low inflation and higher GDP. Traditional economics usually assumes that the goal of economics is to increase wealth, income and profit. However, many people argue that this can lead to a dissatisfied society and social problems.

MONEY CAN'T BUY YOU HAPPINESS

Adjusted for inflation, in 2016 U.S. real GDP was $16,732 billon. In 1947 it was $1,932 billion. Since the Second World War, U.S. real GDP has increased more than eightfold, but are U.S. citizens really any happier?

The Easterlin paradox notes that happiness data are typically static despite rising real income. The problem is that economic growth and rising real output brings many challenges, such as increased congestion, a decline in the affordability of housing, more pollution, higher crime rates, higher inequality and more stress. China's recent economic growth offers a good example — it has averaged close to 10 percent a year, but China has also experienced a rise in problems such as pollution, congestion and the increased stress of seeking more wealth.

Does Higher or Lower GDP Affect Happiness?

⌇ **Increase pollution**
⌇ **Increase congestion**
⌇ **Increase crime**

⌇ **More money for education and health**
⌇ **Higher wages**
⌇ **More investment**

▲ *Between 1957 and 2005, average incomes in the United States almost tripled. Yet self-reported levels of happiness remained constant. In other words, rising incomes did not cause any increase in the number of people saying they were "very happy."*

DIMINISHING MARGINAL UTILITY OF WEALTH

At low levels of GDP per capita, economic growth is likely to have a significant impact on improving satisfaction. Overcoming real poverty enables people to have vastly improved living standards — sufficient food, housing and education are all possible with rising GDP. It would be a mistake to say there is no correlation between GDP and happiness.

However, at a certain point wealth has a diminishing marginal utility. Rising real incomes in the United States may enable people to have two family cars rather than one, but the improvement in satisfaction from having more cars is very marginal. Rising incomes should, in theory, enable people to enjoy more leisure time and lead less stressful lives. However, we have often struggled to achieve this, with the economic growth of recent decades leading to an increase in working hours and stress related to work.

"Today the 'workaholic' rich have replaced the 'idle' rich." Robert Skidelsky and Edward Skidelsky, *How Much Is Enough? The Love of Money and the Case for the Good Life,* 2012.

This is where happiness economics can help prioritize decisions. A society seeking to maximize happiness may decide to limit the average working day, freeing up more time for leisure, as long as we accept the trade-off of lower GDP.

MEASURING HAPPINESS

One challenge for measuring happiness is that it is very subjective. Some people may not enjoy more leisure time and may miss a 45-hour working week. Governments can use surveys and measure indexes such as life expectancy, years of education and quality of environment, but it is not an exact science. Happiness may be a function of a whole range of factors, such as political freedom, national identity and quality of relationships — all factors outside the traditional scope of economics. The important contribution of happiness economics is to emphasize that living standards depend on much more than easily measurable economic statistics.

CHAPTER 8

FINANCIAL ECONOMICS

MONEY — FUNCTION AND USES

Money is essentially a medium of exchange. It is something individuals are willing to accept as payment for goods and services. If it is accepted as a medium of exchange, it will also have other uses.

"Money's a matter of functions four, a Medium, a Measure, a Standard, a Store." This couplet gives us the four functions of money:

- Medium of exchange: using money to buy goods.
- Measure of value: goods can be priced in monetary terms.
- Standard of deferred payment: for example, a mortgage with a monthly repayment of $500.
- Store of value or wealth: money can be saved in a bank to be used when needed.

In primitive economies, there was no need for money. Hunters would catch their food, and perhaps barter a sheep for a cowhide. Often there was no bartering, with communities simply giving to those in need — with the expectation that the favor would be returned when needed.

But as economies developed and people began trading with different communities, certain metals became a convenient way to pay for an increasingly diverse range of goods. Precious metal is a form of commodity money because it has intrinsic value. If you cut a gold coin in half, it is worth half as much. In fact, in the Middle Ages you often had to pay with weighing scales to hand to make sure people hadn't chipped the edges off their gold coins to make a few extra.

DEVELOPMENT OF MONEY AND BANKING

As economies developed, it became increasingly difficult to carry around piles of gold coins. Instead, merchants and banks issued promissory notes or paper money. During the Crusades, it was

a logistical challenge to carry sufficient gold to pay your army. It was during this period that the Knights Templar developed a form of banking system. In place of gold, they issued check of guarantee that could be exchanged for gold in other countries where the Knights Templar had influence.

Over time, central banks started issuing paper money, with the promise that it could be converted to gold. In practice, people had faith in the paper money and rarely asked to convert it.

GOLD STANDARD
· · · · · · · · ·

There have been varying forms of gold standard but the principle is that the value of a currency is linked to the supply of gold. If money is convertible to gold, it is less likely to lose value through inflation. You can print money, but you can't print gold. During the Great Depression, deflation and falling output encouraged countries to abandon the gold standard and use nonconvertible fiat money (see page 242).

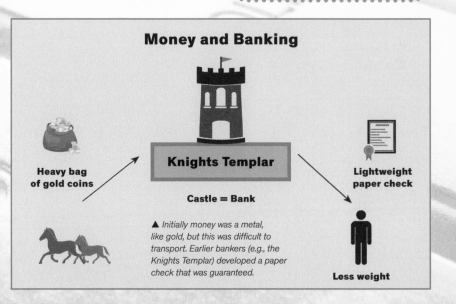

Money and Banking

Heavy bag of gold coins

Knights Templar

Castle = Bank

Lightweight paper check

Less weight

▲ Initially money was a metal, like gold, but this was difficult to transport. Earlier bankers (e.g., the Knights Templar) developed a paper check that was guaranteed.

FIAT MONEY

Fiat is a Latin word meaning "let there be." The idea of fiat money is that the government and central bank simply state that the paper money they print is legal tender and can be used as a means of payment. Fiat money has no intrinsic value (unlike gold). If people lose confidence in the government decree, money would have no use.

With fiat money (again, unlike gold), there is the possibility of inflation. If a government prints more fiat money, the increase in money supply will (in normal circumstances) cause a decline in the value of money.

Fiat Money

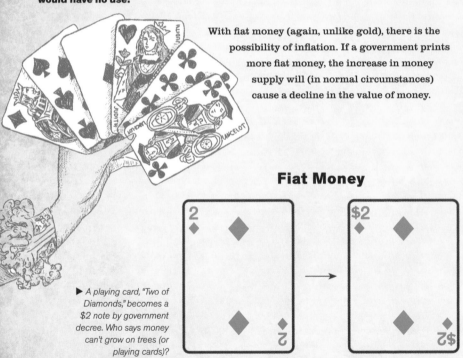

▶ A playing card, "Two of Diamonds," becomes a $2 note by government decree. Who says money can't grow on trees (or playing cards)?

In the 17th century in New France (now part of Canada), the governor, Jacques de Meulles, found himself with a shortage of coins. Facing the prospect of a mutinous army, he improvised a novel solution — he took away all the playing cards, wrote a value on them and signed them. Despite its obvious ad hoc nature, the cards were widely accepted in the colony as a medium of exchange. For several years, people were paid in card money and it was used in place of "real" coins.

However, it didn't have a happy ending, as the Seven Years' War with Britain led to rapid inflation and the card money was devalued. People hoarded gold and tried to use the card money to make payments instead. In 1763 the French government agreed to convert the remaining card money into debentures, but unfortunately the French government was bankrupt and these debentures became worthless.

MONEY IN PRISONS
• • • • • • • • • •

In prison, a commodity like cigarettes often becomes the unofficial currency. Why?

- Cigarette supply is limited to a daily ration — there is little chance of inflation.
- Cigarettes have intrinsic value to smokers.
- They were widely accepted in an era when most people smoked.
- They could be stored without losing value.

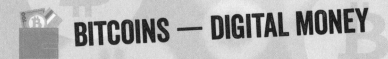

BITCOINS — DIGITAL MONEY

We are used to fiat money regulated by a government. If you make a bank transfer from your account to someone else's, the bank acts as an intermediary, electronically debiting your account and crediting the other person's account. The banking system is also overseen by a monetary authority such as a central bank. However, we have seen that if you are in prison, there is nothing to stop you creating your own form of currency — cigarettes. You don't need an intermediary.

The principle of digital money is the same. It is a form of money created by its users without a central authority to oversee and regulate it. Initially, the bitcoin system created 21 million bitcoins, which will be slowly released until an estimated date of 2140. This means there is a finite number of bitcoins. You gain bitcoins by buying them with cash or providing a service. Then you can use your bitcoins to pay for a service or good from other users who have faith in the bitcoin system. You can also "mine" bitcoins by solving complex math equations. Bitcoin transactions are registered on an open-source system so that when you pay for a service, your bitcoins are taken from your account and given to someone else. This transaction is publically recorded and marked on the ledger — all users can see what has happened.

Bitcoins are sometimes referred to as a peer-to-peer system in the sense that transactions occur between two individuals without any third-party intermediary, though each transaction is overseen by a decentralized network of users. Some people claim that using bitcoins is like being able to send a gold coin by email. For others, it is a highly volatile system with no guarantee of its long-term viability.

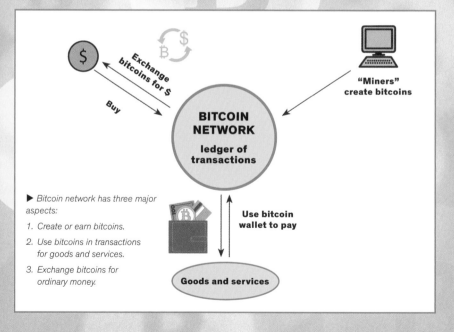

"Miners" create bitcoins

Exchange bitcoins for $

Buy

BITCOIN NETWORK
ledger of transactions

Use bitcoin wallet to pay

Goods and services

▶ Bitcoin network has three major aspects:
1. Create or earn bitcoins.
2. Use bitcoins in transactions for goods and services.
3. Exchange bitcoins for ordinary money.

BOND MARKET

The bond market is a financial market on which debt is bought and sold. The most important bond market is for government debt. The reaction of the bond market can have a very powerful influence on economic policy. In 1993, James Carville, an adviser to U.S. President Bill Clinton, stated: "I used to think if there was reincarnation, I wanted to come back as the president or the pope ... But now I want to come back as the bond market. You can intimidate everybody."

HOW IT WORKS

If the government spends more than it receives in tax revenue, it will need to make up the shortfall. To raise funds it sells government bonds, such as U.S. Treasury bonds, which are bought by the private sector (individuals, pension funds and so on). Suppose an investor buys a $1000 government bond, and in return gets an interest rate on the bond of 5 percent a year. (The government will also repay the $1,000 at the end of the bond term of 10 years.) The government raises money by selling bonds, and investors get a safe investment and a guaranteed nominal interest rate (see Glossary).

BOND PRICES AND BOND YIELDS

You can buy bonds directly from the government, but there is also a secondary market on which the initial buyer can sell on to others — you may not want to wait 10 years to get your initial $1,000 back. The effective interest rate on a bond can vary. Suppose we start off

BOND VALUE

	Annual Payment	Yield	
$1,000 @ 5%	$50	5%	2000
$1,200	$50	4.1%	2001
$800	$50	6.2%	2002

↓ Increase demand for bonds

↓ Decrease demand for bonds

Inverse relationship

Price / Yield

Price / Yield

▲ *$1,000 bond has annual payment of $50 (5%). If the price of a bond rises to $1,200, the effective yield falls to 4.1%. If the price of a bond falls to $800, the effective yield rises to 6.2%. As bond prices fall, the effective yield becomes greater and vice versa.*

with a $1,000 bond at 5 percent. The government will pay $50 a year in interest. But if bonds become popular, more investors will want to buy them. This causes the price of bonds to rise. Suppose the price of bonds rises to $1,200. The government still pays $50, so the effective interest rate is now 4.17 percent.

In other words, as the price of bonds rises (because of higher demand), the bond yield falls.

WHAT HAPPENS IF PEOPLE START SELLING BONDS?

Suppose investors become nervous about the future liquidity of a government (if, for example, there is a very high budget deficit). Investors may start to sell bonds on the bond market. If supply increases, the price of bonds will fall. If those $1,000 bonds fall in value to $500, the effective interest rate is now $50/500 = 10 percent. In other words, a fall in the price of bonds leads to a higher bond yield. Another way of thinking about it is that if government bonds are seen as more risky, investors will demand a higher interest rate to compensate.

WHAT FACTORS DETERMINE BOND YIELDS?

There are many factors that can determine bond yields:

Prospect of debt default. If investors think a government may default on its debts, they will worry about losing part or all of their investment. This fear would cause bond yields to rise as the investors sell their bonds. Countries like Argentina, Russia and Greece have all seen sharp rises in bond yields because of some form of default. Countries like the United States and the United Kingdom with no history of debt default, can generally benefit from relatively low bond yields.

Inflation. If the interest rate on bonds is 5 percent and inflation is 2 percent, an investor gets a real interest rate of 3 percent — a good rate of return. However, suppose inflation increases to 10 percent. This is bad news for bond investors because the interest rate of 5 percent is insufficient to cover the decline in value of money resulting from inflation of 10 percent. Investors will not want to hold a bond with an interest rate of 5 percent when inflation is 10 percent. Investors will sell, the price of bonds will go down and bond yields will go up. Inflation is seen as a partial default. Governments can make it easier to pay off their debts by allowing inflation, but investors will be less willing to buy bonds in the future.

Economic growth. Investors can choose where to invest their money. If they are optimistic about the economy, they may invest in the stock market and buy corporate bonds. Shares and corporate bonds tend to be more risky, but they can give better returns than government bonds. In a recession, with companies more likely to make a loss, investors will prefer the security of government bonds — demand will rise and the interest rate will fall.

Interest rates. If the central bank raises interest rates, it becomes more attractive

to save money in a bank. You don't need to buy government bonds if you can get a good rate of return by simply saving. Therefore, bond yields will closely follow commercial interest rates. One of the main reasons why bond yields are so low in 2016 is that commercial interest rates are also very low.

REASONS FOR FALLING BOND YIELDS

Over the past decade, global bond yields have tended to fall, for various reasons:

- A fall in global inflation.
- Low rates of economic growth.
- An excess of surplus saving in the world. People have a lot of savings, but there is a shortage of good investment options. Therefore, people have become

willing to buy government bonds even at very low interest rates.

- Greater demand for less risky assets.
- Demographics: more pensioners are investing their savings, causing greater demand for bonds.
- Unconventional monetary policy: quantitative easing involves the creation of money and the central bank purchasing government bonds, which further drives down interest rates.

CREDIT RATING AGENCIES

Agencies such as Moody's and Standard & Poor's (S&P) give a rating to the credit worthiness of government bonds (and corporate bonds). If they feel there is no risk of default, they may give an AAA rating. This AAA rating is highly prized and will help make it cheaper to sell these bonds. If credit rating agencies have a negative opinion on the credit worthiness of a government, then they will reduce the rating to BBB or CCC. BB or CCC is usually considered "junk bond" status. This means there is a likelihood of default.

A rating downgrade can be a political blow, as it is a negative signal about government debt. However, the usefulness of credit rating agencies is questioned. Before the credit crunch, many mortgage securities received AAA ratings, but after the credit crunch, they were rapidly reclassified as "junk bond" status. It shows that the credit rating agencies may not know any more than the market.

▶ A bull market means prices of assets are rising. For the past 30 years there has been a bull bond market — with rising prices of bonds and falling interest rates.

Caption to some

STOCK MARKET

The stock market plays an important role in the economy and can be seen as a very rough barometer of economic well-being.

THE ROLE OF THE STOCK MARKET

Most large companies are public limited companies (PLCs), which means anyone can buy shares in those companies. Buying shares means you may receive dividends (a share of the company's profit), and if the company is successful and its share price rises, you will benefit from capital gains. Of course, the reverse is true — if a company goes out of business, you can lose everything. Shares are a more risky investment than saving with a bank, but they can give better returns.

For companies, selling shares is an effective way to raise money for investment. Unlike a bank loan, a company is not obliged to pay investors a set interest rate straight away. It can defer the payment of dividends until the company is more profitable. For example, to finance a long-term investment project like the Eurotunnel a company needs to raise billions of euros to cover construction costs and so on. Many investors bought shares knowing that they might not receive dividends for years to come.

HOW DOES THE ECONOMY AFFECT THE STOCK MARKET?

If an economy experiences low inflation and high economic growth, this is, all things being equal, generally good news

▼ Eurotunnel, founded in 1986, raised money from shareholders to fund the £9 billion ($11.6 billion) cost of building a tunnel between France and the United Kingdom.

for the stock market. **Higher growth will lead to greater profitability and companies will be able to increase dividend payments, attracting more investors and pushing up the share price. In a recession, profits fall and companies may go bankrupt. This reduces demand for shares as dividends and capital values are likely to fall. However, in the real world, we often find that the stock market behaves in a counterintuitive way. Share prices can rise in a recession and fall in a period of economic growth.**

WHY SHARE PRICES RISE DURING A RECESSION

Investors are always looking ahead. If the economy is in recession, investors may start buying shares in anticipation of an economic recovery. Similarly, if the economy is doing well, it may be a good time to cash in on your capital gains.

In 2007–16, we saw a low rate of global economic growth, but, ironically, company profitability has increased. Over this period, companies have been able to keep wage growth low, which increases their profit margin. Therefore, share prices have done relatively well.

The global economy in 2007–16 also saw very low interest rates, with some government bonds having negative interest rates. Therefore, investors have looked to the stock market to get a better rate of interest in the form of dividends.

IS A RISING STOCK MARKET A SIGN OF ECONOMIC SUCCESS?

During Barack Obama's term as U.S. President (2008–16) the stock market rose — but you have to be careful when using the stock market as a marker of economic success. The rise in the stock market over that period is at least partly due to a global savings glut, quantitative easing and an unprecedented period of record low interest rates.

Investing on the stock market is risky, but it may be a risk worth taking when government bonds offer so little value.

Another feature of the stock market is that prices can be driven by "market sentiment," which can swing from excessive optimism to deeply rooted bearishness (see Glossary). For example, in the late 1990s we saw irrational exuberance for the shares of IT-related companies, which led to the dot-com bubble (see Irrational Exuberance, page 148).

STOCK MARKET CRASHES

A well-known joke says that the stock market has predicted nine out of the last five recessions. The point is that a rapid fall in share prices can sometimes lead to a recession. But we may sometimes see a 20 percent drop in share prices that does not result in recession, but rather continued economic growth. A fall in share prices may indicate a decline in underlying health of an economy — and it may not!

In theory at least, a fall in share prices will adversely affect the economy. Falling share prices lead to a decline in wealth and this may reduce some consumption, though the link is relatively weak — investors who put money into the stock market generally have other forms of savings and income. A prolonged fall

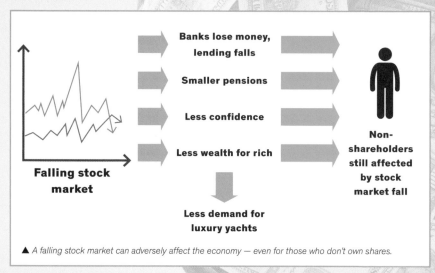

▲ A falling stock market can adversely affect the economy — even for those who don't own shares.

1987 SHARE-PRICE CRASH

A good example of the stock market not affecting the economy is the "Black Monday" October 1987 crash. Within a week, share prices around the world fell 20 percent. Even now people argue about what caused this rapid drop, with some suggesting it was due to obscure "technical factors." The stock market crash certainly caused a lot of concern — some people were worried that there would be a repeat of the 1929 Wall Street Crash and subsequent Great Depression. Policymakers took it seriously and interest rates were cut. But, ultimately, there was no recession, share prices recovered, and the fall in share prices had no link to economic performance. This shows that temporary falls in share prices may have only a very limited impact on direct consumption. People don't rely on share-price performance to fund their everyday spending. It also shows that stock markets can move as a result of changes in market sentiment that are not necessarily related to market fundamentals.

in share prices will reduce the value of investment trusts and pension funds, leading to lower pension annuities for retirees. Even people who don't directly invest in the stock market are affected by investments in pension funds. Furthermore, a rapid drop in share prices may reduce consumer confidence and perhaps business confidence (see Glossary). It will be harder for companies to raise money on the stock market and may lead to a decline in investment.

1929 WALL STREET CRASH

The 1929 Wall Street Crash is famous — or perhaps infamous — for being the precursor of the Great Depression.

Economic confidence ballooned during the so-called Roaring Twenties. There was a rapid rise in living standards with ordinary workers able to afford a car for the first time. This growth was at least partly due to real improvements in

technology and working practices. However, the economic growth and easy monetary policy (U.S. interest rates were low at the time) fueled an irrational exuberance in financial markets. People believed the stock market was a one-way bet — a surefire way of increasing their wealth. Share prices rose continually in the 1920s, encouraging more investors to try their luck.

Investors started to buy shares on the margin, which, in simple terms, meant borrowing to buy more shares than they could afford. The trick was to buy on the margin and wait for share prices to rise before selling, which brought greater capital gains than "ordinary" share buying. In 1929, there were innumerable "paper millionaires" — people who had bought shares on the margin and seen share prices rise.

However, share prices had become divorced from economic growth and the actual profits made by companies. By the late 1920s, the U.S. economy started to see a recession in agriculture and profit growth was much lower than share-price growth. After a series of companies reported lower-than-expected profits, investors started to think this was a good time to cash in on their gains. There was a very rapid shift in market sentiment — having previously expected prices to keep rising, now everyone wanted to sell. Share prices fell, which panicked other investors into selling too.

The real losers were those who had borrowed to buy shares — which were now worth less than they had been bought for. As share prices fell, people who couldn't pay back their creditors went bankrupt. Banks started to lose money and wanted to call in their loans, but because share prices had fallen, many loans had to be written off.

The economic damage precipitated by the Wall Street Crash lasted through most of the 1930s.

GREAT DEPRESSION

The Great Depression saw an unprecedented global drop in output and period of mass unemployment.

Even before the Wall Street Crash of 1929 there were problems that threatened to undermine the apparent boom of the Jazz Age. U.S. agriculture was already in recession, struggling with low prices and oversupply.

In 1925 the United Kingdom reentered the gold standard (see page 241) at an overvalued rate and experienced deflation because exports were uncompetitive and imports cheap. In response to UK deflation, the United States ran a looser monetary policy in order to reduce the value of the dollar. But this loose monetary policy contributed to a credit bubble.

After the Wall Street Crash, falling share prices led to a rise in personal bankruptcy and bad loans, causing banks to lose money. The financial panic of 1929 also filtered through to the wider public, even affecting those who didn't own shares. News of bank losses caused savers to queue up to withdraw their money. But banks soon ran out, and images of long queues of people unable to take out their savings led to a classic "run on the banks."

In the United States in the 1930s there was no lender of last resort (a central bank willing to offer liquidity), so many local banks went bankrupt, causing people to lose their savings. This only caused more panic and a further loss of confidence in the banking sector. In 1930 alone, over 700 U.S. banks went bankrupt. This contributed to a precipitous fall in the money supply and economic activity.

Bank failures also caused investment to dry up and many workers were made redundant. The rise in unemployment caused a further fall in demand, creating a negative multiplier effect (see page 132).

The rise in unemployment brought about protectionist policies — governments around the world increased tariffs to protect domestic jobs. But higher global tariffs led to a decline in trade and fall in global exports, exacerbating the fall in domestic demand.

In the early 1930s, governments were reluctant to engineer any increase in demand — the economic orthodoxy of the time believed in the necessity of balanced budgets. Many governments increased taxes and cut government spending in order to balance their budgets, but this only caused a further fall in demand.

In the mid-1930s, there was a partial recovery in the United States, helped by New Deal spending during the presidency of Franklin D. Roosevelt. It was only with the onset of the Second World War that military spending rose sufficiently to produce a fall in unemployment.

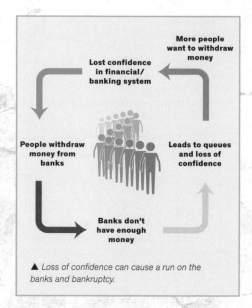

▲ Loss of confidence can cause a run on the banks and bankruptcy.

◀ Bank loans increased during the 1920s to a peak of $9.7 billion, but then fell sharply during the Great Depression with a period of bank closures (1929–33).

HOUSING MARKET

The 2000s saw a remarkable boom in house prices in the U.S. and Canada, followed by a sharp crash by decade's end. They have since continued to rise. How did a long-term investment such as a house create a speculative bubble not unlike that of stocks and commodities?

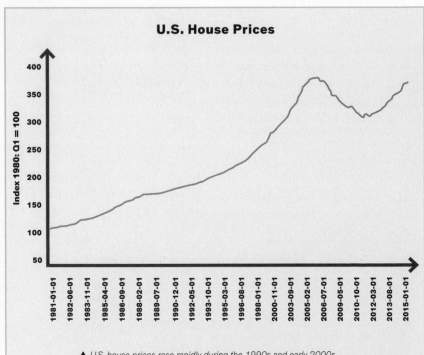

U.S. House Prices

Index 1980: Q1 = 100

▲ *U.S. house prices rose rapidly during the 1990s and early 2000s, before falling between 2006 and 2012, only to rise again.*

In the 1980s and 1990s, many financial markets were deregulated, enabling banks to be more involved in both deposit and investment banking. There was also a growing culture of taking greater risks to increase profits and growth.

The strong economy and rising incomes of the 1990s and 2000s encouraged individuals to buy houses. Strong economic growth combined with low inflation created a sense of economic stability. This encouraged banks and financial institutions to be creative in expanding their range of mortgages. Lending more enabled them to increase their profitability.

Previously, banks were strict in lending to people with good credit histories and proof of a sufficient income to meet mortgage payments. But in the 2000s, mortgage companies relaxed these criteria. Mortgage brokers often received bonuses for selling mortgages — so they had less incentive to evaluate whether or not borrowers could afford them in the long term.

Compared to the 1980s, interest rates were low in the late 1990s and 2000s. After the economy wobbled in the wake of 9/11, the Federal Reserve responded by cutting interest rates to a record low of 1 percent in 2003. Low borrowing costs made buying a house very attractive compared to renting. These rates were then increased to over 5 percent by 2006.

THE HOUSING CRASH

This cycle of rising prices — encouraging more lending and greater demand and further pushing up prices — ended abruptly in 2005. First, the Federal Reserve, worried about an overheating economy and the prospect of inflation, started to increase interest rates. By historical standards, interest rates were still low, but many borrowers had taken out very large mortgages as a percentage of their incomes, and even

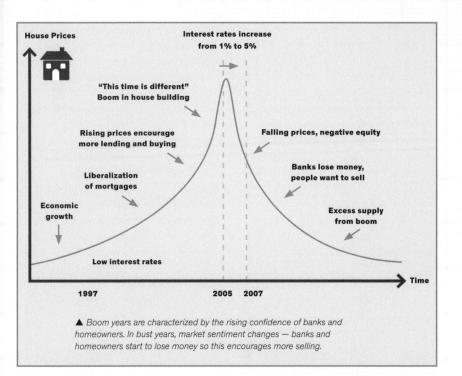

House Prices

Interest rates increase
from 1% to 5%

"This time is different"
Boom in house building

Rising prices encourage
more lending and buying

Falling prices, negative equity

Liberalization
of mortgages

Banks lose money,
people want to sell

Economic
growth

Excess supply
from boom

Low interest rates

Time

1997   2005 2007

▲ *Boom years are characterized by the rising confidence of banks and homeowners. In bust years, market sentiment changes — banks and homeowners start to lose money so this encourages more selling.*

BOOM

1. Liberalization of mortgages
2. Rising prices encourage more lending and buying
3. Boom in house building
4. "This time is different"

BUST

1. Interest rates increase
2. Falling prices: people want to sell
3. Banks lose money: don't want to lend
4. Excess supply from boom years

a modest rise in interest rates led to a big increase in monthly interest payments — which they now couldn't afford.

This rise in interest rates was exacerbated when introductory mortgage rates came to an end and mortgage rates started to increase on top of the Federal Reserve's interest rate rise. Due to the change in the economic climate, banks saw a rapid rise in mortgage defaults. They started to lose money and in response reduced their lending.

Homeowners unable to meet mortgage payments started to put their houses on the market. The increase in supply caused prices to fall. With prices falling, other speculators sought to cash in on their capital gains before prices fell further. As prices fell, the whole dynamic of the housing market changed. Mortgage companies no longer wanted to lend because they were concerned about the rise in defaults and their marketing strategies were reliant on rising house prices.

The fall in house prices was exacerbated by the boom in home building that occurred toward the end of 2005. Home builders were left with thousands of houses they couldn't sell. Due to widespread default on mortgages, banks repossessed many homes but were left with negative equity (see Glossary). It is not surprising that, with a collapse in demand and an increase in the number of houses for sale, prices fell.

▼ *Rising interest rates caused mortgage defaults and negative equity. Many homeowners lost their houses during the housing crash.*

THE GEOGRAPHY OF FALLING HOUSE PRICES

House-price falls were not evenly spread across the United States. The biggest falls came in areas that had seen the biggest boom in prices and home-building, such as Florida. The boom and bust was also seen across the world — Spain and Ireland, for example, experienced a collapse in house prices after a similar boom. In the United Kingdom, house prices fell in 2008 but recovered more quickly, and by 2016 were higher than their 2007 peak. This is because there has never been a boom in home-building in the United Kingdom. Even though house prices were overvalued, there was still a shortage of housing.

People felt the housing market was not vulnerable to a crash (as commodities were) because people will always need somewhere to live. In fact, many senior analysts were optimistic about the prospects of the housing market. As late as June 2005, Alan Greenspan, then Chairman of the Federal Reserve, was unsure that there was a bust on the way: "Although a 'bubble' in home prices for the nation as a whole does not appear likely there do appear to be, at a minimum, signs of froth in some local markets."

However, with the benefit of hindsight, this froth was the last stage of an unsustainable boom and the global economy would soon suffer from a painful readjustment process.

THIS TIME IT'S (NOT) DIFFERENT

John Templeton was right (again): "The four most dangerous words in investing are, 'This time it's different.'" This was not the first time there had been a boom and bust in asset values. The interesting thing is the psychology of people involved — although house-price-to-income ratios were rising rapidly, people ignored potential warning signs of an overheating market.

CREDIT CRUNCH

The credit crunch of 2007–2008 was a sequence of events that led to a shortage of money in the financial system, causing banks to be short of liquidity and in some cases to go out of business. The credit crunch was a real shock to financial markets and the global economy. The cause of the credit crunch was linked very closely to the housing boom and the behavior of mortgage companies.

To increase their mortgage lending and therefore profitability, mortgage companies borrowed from banks. To do so they created complex financial instruments called collateralized debt obligations (CDOs), which were essentially "mortgage bundles." Sales of CDOs rose from $30 billion in 2003 to $225 billion in 2006.

Banks around the world bought these mortgage bundles, effectively lending money to U.S. mortgage companies. The banks thought they were buying a profitable investment, not realizing the extent to which these mortgage bundles were tied up with risky subprime lending.

When the U.S. housing market crashed and people defaulted on their mortgage repayments, mortgage companies lost money. In theory, that is where the problem should have ended. But "reputable" banks around the world were highly exposed to the U.S. mortgage industry. Indirectly, they had lent money to the U.S. subprime mortgage industry. Therefore, the U.S. mortgage defaults

directly affected European banks (whose own mortgage-lending criteria were generally stricter). They lost a lot of money.

Another feature of the financial system in the early 2000s was that banks increasingly borrowed on money markets (see Glossary) to finance their lending. In a traditional banking system, a bank would lend a percentage of its customers' deposits. But due to deregulation and the desire to grow, banks often borrowed short-term loans on money markets at low interest rates. In other words,

banks borrowed from other financial institutions in order to lend. This may sound strange, but money markets were (for a time) very stable, with low interest rates, and such borrowing was considered standard practice.

When mortgage defaults started to increase, however, many financial institutions lost money. When banks lost money, they needed to try to improve their liquidity (increasing the amount of cash they had). So they cut back on loans and tried to encourage deposits.

U.S. mortgage company

Subprime customers

Lend money

Banks gain CDOs (mortgage bundles)

International banks

◀ Banks around the world were indirectly funding the boom in U.S. subprime mortgage lending. U.S. mortgage companies borrowed from other banks to be able to lend more.

Banks that relied on borrowing from these money markets to maintain liquidity suddenly found that they could no longer gain sufficient liquidity — nobody wanted to lend and the money markets effectively shrank.

Suddenly the market realized that no investment was safe, including money deposited in banks. When people don't trust banks, they want to withdraw their money. But the banking system can't cope if everyone wants to withdraw their money at the same time.

There was a renewed fear of a run on the banks — not seen since the 1930s. Governments around the world had to offer reassurances that they would act as lenders of last resort. In the United Kingdom, the government had to

LEHMAN BROTHERS

• • • • • • • • • •

Lehman Brothers was a U.S. investment bank that experienced this shortage of liquidity acutely. In October 2008, it was faced with the fact that it had completely run out of liquidity. Surprisingly, the Federal Reserve and government didn't intervene. They basically said "bad luck," and Lehman Brothers went out of business. Anyone who had invested with Lehman Brothers lost everything.

invest £50 billion to save and effectively nationalize some major commercial banks.

The biggest problem of the credit crunch was that companies and individuals found it very difficult to get any type of loan. Banks didn't have the

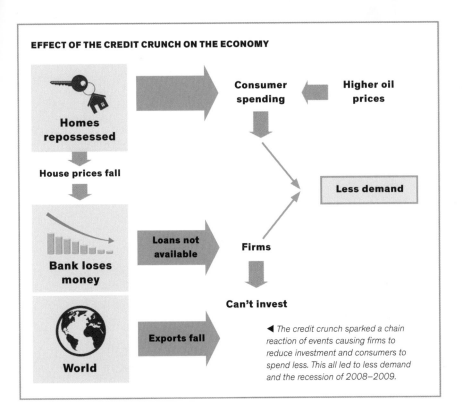

EFFECT OF THE CREDIT CRUNCH ON THE ECONOMY

Homes repossessed

House prices fall

Bank loses money

World

Consumer spending ← Higher oil prices

Loans not available → Firms

Exports fall

Less demand

Can't invest

◀ The credit crunch sparked a chain reaction of events causing firms to reduce investment and consumers to spend less. This all led to less demand and the recession of 2008–2009.

ability to lend. They needed to recover loans, rather than lend more. Most companies rely on the ability to borrow to finance investment. As lending dried up, companies cut back on investment and this led to a fall in the rate of economic growth.

There were other factors affecting the economy in 2007 and 2008 — such as the fall in confidence, rising oil prices and higher inflation — but the biggest problem was the near freeze in bank lending, which caused a sudden drop in business and economic activity. This caused the deepest recession since the 1930s.

CHAPTER 9

GLOBAL ECONOMY

GLOBALIZATION

Globalization refers to the increasing integration and interdependence of national economies. It reflects a general move toward "one world" in which national boundaries are less significant.

Globalization is also quite a vague concept, enabling both supporters and detractors to frame it as either very beneficial or as the source of the many ills facing the world. However, most people agree that globalization has certain features:

- Greater trade due to the removal of tariff barriers.
- Migration of labor across national boundaries.
- Growth of multinational companies.
- Economies that are more closely linked, creating a global economic cycle.
- Global solutions for economic and social issues such as global warming.

Globalization is not a new phenomenon. People have been moving around the world since the first humans migrated from Africa. When Marco Polo discovered an early trade route to China, he was an early pioneer

```
              Multinational
               companies

New communication
and transport              Trade

                 🌐

Production              Tax avoidance
Specialization
around world

              Labor
             migration
```

◀ *Aspects of globalization.*

of globalization. But the process of globalization has undoubtedly sped up over the past 50 years. What has caused this acceleration of globalization?

Growth in free trade. The general trend of the past 50 years has been to cut tariff barriers and encourage trade between countries.

Growth of new economies. The past 20–30 years have seen the emergence of many powerful new economies, such as those of China, India and Brazil, creating new export markets and causing a shift in patterns of production from the developed world to emerging economies.

Technology. Satellite and internet communication have enabled, among other things, real-time phone and video conferencing, and business travel is also much easier and quicker.

Containerization. Sometimes the biggest improvements almost go unnoticed because they seem so low-tech. But it is argued that the adoption of the standard shipping container revolutionized trade — more so than modern technologies such as the Internet.

PROS	CONS
• Improved trade, increased income • Decreased poverty, especially in Southeast Asia • Migration of labor, increased income for workers in poor countries • Increased income and wealth	• Free trade not always good for developing inequality • Still poverty (especially in Africa) and inequality • Downward pressure on wages for unskilled workers in the West • Increased environmental problems

Critics of globalization argue that it is responsible for exacerbating many of the world's economic and social problems. In *Making Globalization Work* (2006), the Nobel Prize–winning American economist Joseph Stiglitz said that, "Globalization had succeeded in unifying people from around the world — against globalization. Factory workers in the United States saw their jobs being threatened by competition from China. Farmers in developing countries saw their jobs being threatened by the highly subsidized corn and other crops from the United States."

Globalization benefits the developed world more than developing economies. For example, many developing economies remain dependent on low-growth, primary products (see Glossary), while developed countries benefit from outsourcing labor-intensive work to countries with lower labor costs. Similarly, the increased environmental degradation caused by globalization has primarily affected developing economies. It is easier for the developed world to import raw materials from environmentally sensitive areas such as the Amazon rainforest.

Globalization has enabled multinational companies to benefit from tax avoidance by registering in low-tax countries such as Bermuda and Luxembourg (while benefitting from public services in the countries in which they do business). Tax avoidance has contributed to a huge growth in the cash reserves of major U.S. companies held in offshore accounts.

Globalization also has critics in the developed world, with many people feeling that globalization has led to job losses in manufacturing industries as work is outsourced to countries with lower labor costs. Globalization is often blamed for downward pressure on wages, especially for unskilled workers.

IS GLOBALIZATION REALLY THE SOURCE OF ALL PROBLEMS?

Supporters of globalization argue that it has led to rising income levels in poor countries. Foreign investment has increased capital investment and created new jobs. Even if very low paid, the jobs are usually an improvement on subsistence agricultural work. In recent decades, many emerging economies have seen a rise in living standards, enabling millions to escape poverty.

It is true that there are many real environmental problems — however, it is a mistake to blame it all on globalization. The problem is not the process of globalization but a lack of concerted action. You could argue that what is needed is more globalization — more global cooperation and agreements to manage resources in a sustainable way.

Globalization is often used as a scapegoat for other issues, such as global poverty, environmental issues and unemployment. However, the process of globalization is hard to reverse, and even if it could be reversed, it wouldn't solve the underlying issues of global poverty and environmental degradation.

FREE TRADE

For some economists, free trade is the holy grail and the cornerstone of their economic philosophy. Yet, while economists are more or less united in seeing the benefits of free trade, increasingly it has become politically unpopular, with many people blaming free trade for widening inequality and a decline in living standards. So why do economists generally speak highly of free trade?

BENEFITS OF FREE TRADE

Without trade, countries would have to produce everything they need. Free trade enables countries to specialize in areas in which they have a comparative advantage — in other words, they produce the goods and provide the services that they are best at producing and providing relative to other countries. For example, China specializes in labor-intensive manufacturing. The United States increasingly specializes in service-sector industries, such as high-tech IT development and financial services.

It is not practical for a country to try to produce everything it consumes because some industries have significant economies of scale. Belgium, for example, specializes in chocolate production and uses its export revenue to import a small number of airplanes. This specialization enables greater efficiency because countries can concentrate on doing a small number of things well — rather than trying to do everything inefficiently.

In *The Wealth of Nations* (1776), Adam Smith made an analogy between the economy of a household and that of a country: "It is the maxim of every prudent master of a family, never to attempt to make at home what it will cost him more to make than to buy." As a householder, you don't try to produce everything. You specialize, and import goods that it is cheaper to buy than to make yourself — just as countries do.

THE NORTH AMERICAN FREE TRADE AGREEMENT (NAFTA)

NAFTA is a free-trade agreement between Mexico, Canada and the United States. The agreement has encouraged some U.S. companies to move production from the United States to Mexico, which enables

them to reduce labor costs and prices and increase profitability — good news for U.S. companies. It is good news for the Mexican economy too, which receives investment and benefits from a higher demand for labor. However, some argue, it leads to job losses for U.S. workers and a decline in U.S. wages.

On the positive side, the U.S. consumer will benefit from the cheaper prices of goods made in Mexico. This gives them more disposable income with which to buy more goods in other sectors of the economy. The problem is that these small increases in demand for other goods are much less noticeable than the very visible job losses caused by companies moving to Mexico.

NAFTA has helped to raise the incomes of Mexican workers and this has led to a growing Mexican middle class, which has increased demand for U.S. exports. Also, by raising the wages of Mexican workers, it helps to reduce the incentive for migration from Mexico to the United States.

Nor should the reverse side of free trade be forgotten. It is not just about U.S. companies moving the production of goods to Mexico. The United States also exports to NAFTA countries. Excluding oil, the United States has a trade surplus on manufacturing and agricultural goods sold to Mexico. Some U.S. workers have lost out to free trade, but others have benefited from working in industries that export to NAFTA countries.

PROTECTIONISM

Protectionism is a policy of protecting domestic industries from cheap imports, through import tariffs and other measures.

WHAT IS THE MOTIVATION BEHIND PROTECTIONISM AND TARIFFS ON IMPORTS?

The first motivation is revenue. In the early history of the United States, tariffs were a major source of federal revenue. In 1860, tariffs accounted for $53 million (or 95 percent) of federal receipts, though by 2010 that figure had fallen to 1 percent.

The second motivation is to protect domestic jobs. Free trade means some companies won't be able to compete with foreign rivals and may go out of business, which can lead to job losses and regional stagnation. Tariffs are a way to protect companies and whole industries from competition and prevent job losses.

These high-profile closures and job losses are much more striking than the incremental gains for industries that benefit from more exports as part of free-trade deals. If the price of imported vegetables falls 10 percent, most people will not notice. If you are made unemployed because people start importing Japanese cars, you do notice.

In an ideal world we would be able to compensate those who lose their jobs because of free trade by helping them to gain meaningful employment in other, growing industries. However, if there is insufficient help to relocate and retrain workers, free trade will leave certain groups of workers worse off — even if overall there is a net economic gain.

EXAMPLES OF PROTECTIONISM

Tariffs. This is a levy (tax) placed on imported goods. For over 16 years, the European Union had very high tariffs on imports of bananas from Latin America, at €176 per tonne. This was dubbed the "Banana Wars."

Domestic subsidies. If a government gives generous subsidies to a domestic industry, this can be seen as a form of unfair competition and protectionism.

For example, European governments subsidizing the airline industry, or the Chinese government subsidizing their car industry.

Administrative barriers. Different regulations and red tape make it more difficult for foreign companies to trade. This is why the European Union tries to harmonize all laws and regulations within its member states.

Quotas. This is a limit on the quantity of imports from certain countries. In the early 1980s, the United States limited the import of Japanese cars to protect the U.S. car industry. (Though ironically, this limit pushed up the price of Japanese cars and made the Japanese car industry more profitable!)

INFANT INDUSTRY ARGUMENT

The infant industry argument states that new industries in developing economies need some form of protectionism before they can gain sufficient economies of scale to be able to compete in an international setting.

Free trade is usually beneficial for developed economies. However, some economists argue that free trade is disproportionally bad news for emerging economies.

Imagine a country has a comparative advantage in sugar production. As a consequence, 60 percent of its economy and exports are based on sugar. However, there are problems with an economy that revolves around a single commodity.

First, the price of sugar is volatile, and if the price falls, the economy will suffer. A bad year in which prices fall will lead to lower export revenue, falling tax revenues and negative growth.

In the long term there is also likely to be limited growth in the demand for sugar. Even as global incomes rise, wealthier consumers will tend to spend more on clothes, cars and computers rather than sugar for their coffee — the demand this sugar is income inelastic.

For these reasons, there is a good case for a sugar-dependent country to try to diversify its economy and develop other industries — even where it doesn't currently have a comparative advantage. For example, it could try to develop new manufacturing industries that have greater value added (see Glossary).

However, free trade means these new

▲ *An economy based on agricultural products lacks diversity and has limited scope for growth.*

industries will be uncompetitive and will struggle to sell any goods because people will buy cheaper imports. Tariff protection gives a developing country the chance to develop a new industry that can become competitive over time. When the industry is stronger and can exploit economies of scale, it is in a position to deal with free trade and remove tariff barriers.

This suggests that insisting on free trade for all countries at all stages of development is not fair. Many developed countries have had periods of tariff protection (for example, the "Asian Tigers," Hong Kong, Singapore, South Korea and Taiwan, during their economic development), and it is hypocritical to prohibit this measure to other countries.

U.S. PROTECTIONISM IN THE 19TH CENTURY

After the Anglo-American War of 1812 (which ended in 1815!), cheap British imports flooded the U.S. market, threatening the emerging U.S. manufacturing industries. In response, Congress passed new tariffs to discourage British imports in order to help the manufacturing industries to develop.

Throughout the 19th century and early 20th century, the United States retained many tariffs on imports. However, this era of tariff protection coincided with a period of rapid economic growth. It shows how a now developed economy like that of the United States benefited from tariffs in the early stages of its development.

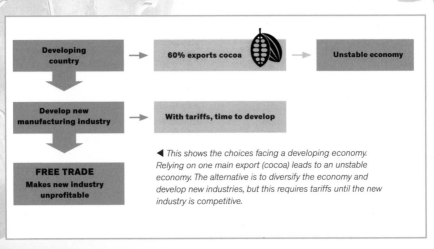

◄ This shows the choices facing a developing economy. Relying on one main export (cocoa) leads to an unstable economy. The alternative is to diversify the economy and develop new industries, but this requires tariffs until the new industry is competitive.

BEGGAR MY NEIGHBOR

Beggar my neighbor is an economic policy that sees a country seek to gain an advantage at the expense of other countries. In the age of mercantilism, this might have meant plundering the gold of a rival empire — you gain and your rival loses (see Mercantilism, page 10).

Modern-day equivalents include imposing tariffs to reduce imports and help domestic industries at the expense of foreign companies. It can also mean an artificial currency devaluation to make exports relatively more competitive, leading to less demand for foreign goods. In the early 2000s it was argued that China's exchange rate was artificially undervalued at the expense of U.S. growth and jobs.

CUTTING CORPORATION TAX

Cutting corporation tax can also be an example of beggar my neighbor. Between 1998 and 2003, Ireland cut its corporation tax rate on trading income (see Glossary) from 32 percent to 12.5 percent. This tax cut was successful in attracting many multinational corporations,

such as Google and Microsoft. Despite the lower tax rate, attracting profitable multinationals helped to increase overall corporation tax revenue. The corporation tax cut is seen as one factor behind the booming Irish economy of the early 2000s. It seems to be a good policy — Ireland benefits from higher tax revenue and more inward investment, and Irish companies get to keep more profit to use for investment.

BEGGAR MY NEIGHBOR

The problem is that while Ireland benefits from increased tax revenue, the United States and other countries lose out because Google and Microsoft are relocating to avoid paying relatively higher tax rates in the United States and Europe (see The Free-Rider Problem, page 58). Furthermore, there is now an

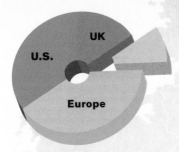

Lower UK tax takes inward investment from Europe

◀ Lower corporation tax attracts investment from one country to another. The United Kingdom gains at Europe's expense, but doesn't increase overall investment. It also creates an incentive for other countries to cut corporation tax to stay competitive.

incentive for other countries to reduce their tax rates to compete with Ireland. In the past decades, there has been a sustained fall in corporation tax rates across the globe, increasing post-tax profits for companies but putting more pressure on the average taxpayer as income tax and sales tax have to go up to compensate.

Attracting inward investment from other countries doesn't increase overall global economic welfare. It merely moves investment from one country to another — low-tax countries benefit at the expense of high-tax countries. However, supporters of corporation tax cuts argue that one benefit is that companies have more retained profit, which enables higher spending on investment. This investment can help develop better products and promote economic growth, (although many multinationals, such as Apple and Google, currently keep a high share of profit in the form of cash, rather than usefully investing it). Apple, for example, has over $200 billion in cash reserves held outside the United States. Higher corporation tax rates in the United States are a motivation for keeping tax offshore.

There is a good case for trying to harmonize global corporation tax rates in order to prevent excessive tax competition. Otherwise we will see a trend of higher taxes for individuals and lower taxes for companies.

GLOBAL SAVINGS GLUT

The global savings glut refers to a situation in which desired saving is greater than desired investment. Essentially, companies and individuals across the world are tending to save rather than invest.

GLOBAL SAVINGS AS A SHARE OF WORLD GDP

The global savings glut has a number of causes.

Economic growth. Growth in developing and emerging economies (see Glossary) has increased the wealth of a new middle class that, as it has become more prosperous, has sought to increase its cash reserves and savings.

Demographic changes. In the United States, baby boomers are starting to save for their upcoming retirements. This demographic shift is occurring in both developed and emerging economies, with an aging global population preferring to save for retirement.

Global uncertainty. The slowdown in global economic growth makes investment less attractive. Economies such as those of Japan, the Eurozone and the United States have seen lower rates of economic growth. This has encouraged investors to put money into safe assets, rather than riskier corporate lending.

Cash hoarding of IT giants. Some of the most successful companies of recent years — Microsoft, Apple and Google — have seen a remarkable rise in cash savings. They are very profitable companies, but they have not seen the need to invest these cash savings.

China's economic policy. China's rapid economic growth has seen a rise in its wealth. It has often sought to keep its currency weak by buying foreign assets, especially U.S. bonds, which is a form of saving.

IS A GLUT OF SAVING A PROBLEM?

In everyday life, saving is seen as a good thing. But the paradox of thrift tells us that excess saving can have unintended consequences for the wider economy (see The Paradox of Thrift, page 126). Some feel that excess savings are at least partly responsible for the low interest rates and asset bubble of the 2000s.

The global savings glut in the 2000s helped to increase demand for all types of bonds. It made it easy for mortgage companies to sell subprime mortgage-based collateralized debt obligations (see Credit Crunch, page 266). It also helped keep interest rates artificially low and encouraged the boom in house prices. In other words, the global savings glut arguably exacerbated the credit bubble of 2000 and the subsequent crash.

With excess demand for savings, demand for government bonds is high. This pushes down the bond yield, and leads to cheaper costs of borrowing for the government.

Savers will see a decline in their return from savings. High demand for saving pushes down interest rates. It is ironic that part of the reason for very low interest rates is that so many people want to save.

The decline in investment has led to a higher share of output retained as profit and distributed to shareholders or saved as cash reserves. For many workers, real wages have been stagnant in the period 2008–16; by contrast, company profitability and cash savings have grown faster than real incomes.

The rise in savings is mixed news. Governments have benefited from lower borrowing costs. People who rely on interest from savings have seen a decline in income.

◀ The impact of a global savings glut is low interest rates, a stronger dollar and rising asset prices (house prices, shares, bonds).

 # THE EURO

The euro is a bold experiment to create a single currency within the Eurozone area (see Glossary). It is currently used by 19 of the 28 member EU states.

The hope was that the European single currency would lead to greater political and economic integration and confer various economic benefits.

Lower transaction costs. If you travel through Europe, it is a great boon to be able to use the same currency in 19 different countries, and tourists save on transaction costs (see Optimal Currency Zone, page 292).

Stable exchange rates. The euro guarantees future exchange rates within European countries. This is good for businesses, which need to know future export and import prices. It was also hoped the stability and lower transaction cost of a single currency would encourage foreign investment, giving, for example, a Japanese firm a greater incentive to set up a factory within the

HISTORY OF THE EURO

• • • • • • • • • • •

1979 onward: Countries join Exchange Rate Mechanism, a semifixed exchange rate system, to prepare for the single currency.

1992: Maastricht Treaty states criteria for European countries to join euro.

1999: Euro comes into existence in virtual form.

2002: Euro notes and coins begin to be circulated, replacing old national currencies.

2010–12: Eurozone crisis — rising bond yields and fiscal crisis in southern Eurozone.

Eurozone in order to benefit from a free-trade area.

Price transparency. With all goods and services denominated in euros it is easy to compare prices between different **European countries**. In theory, this should encourage price competition and be good news for consumers.

In recent years, these benefits of the Euro have been overshadowed by the problems in the Eurozone, which has resulted in the bond crisis and high rates of unemployment. However, the EU is committed to new European Union countries in the East joining the Eurozone — when they meet the criteria of low borrowing and stable exchange rates.

PROBLEMS OF THE EURO

For several years, all seemed well with the euro, but the credit crunch of 2008 precipitated severe challenges to its workings, leading to austerity, recession, high unemployment and a fear that the whole euro project was misguided. What went wrong?

The hope was that the euro would lead to economic convergence — countries would end up with similar rates of inflation and economic growth. But this didn't happen. Countries in southern Europe (Spain, Portugal, Greece) saw higher inflation rates, caused primarily by rising wage costs. This meant that Spanish and Portuguese exports became more expensive than the equivalent

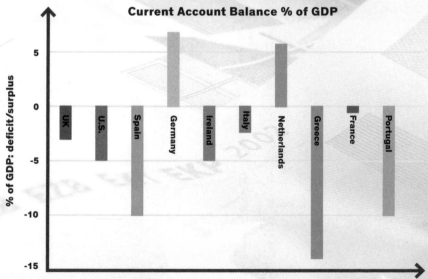

Current Account Balance % of GDP

y-axis: % of GDP: deficit/surplus

Countries (left to right): UK, U.S., Spain, Germany, Ireland, Italy, Netherlands, Greece, France, Portugal

▲ *This shows the size of current account deficit/surplus in selected countries.*

exports from Germany and the Netherlands.

In the past, this would not have been a problem. Before the establishment of the Eurozone, higher inflation in Spain would have caused the Spanish peseta to be devalued against the German deutsche mark in order to restore Spanish competitiveness.

However, this could not happen in the Eurozone – Spain and Portugal could not devalue. That is the whole point of the euro – there are no internal exchange rates. Therefore, Spanish and Portuguese goods became increasingly uncompetitive. This led to record current account deficits.

In 2007, Spain, Greece and Portugal had large current account deficits – 10 percent of GDP or more, an indicator of the divergence in competitiveness that occurred in the Eurozone. This indicates a fundamental disequilibrium in the economy – in these countries the value of imports significantly outweighs the value of exports. It contrasts with Germany and the Netherlands, who have a large current account surplus (their exports are greater than their imports).

The graph below shows that Greece and Spain were uncompetitive and so were importing much more than exporting. This uncompetitiveness led to lower growth in southern Europe.

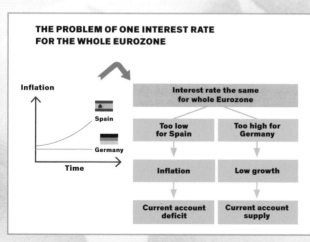

THE PROBLEM OF ONE INTEREST RATE FOR THE WHOLE EUROZONE

◀ Spain has higher inflation than Germany, but both have the same interest rate (set for the whole Eurozone). For Spain, interest rates are too low, leading to inflation and current account deficit. For Germany, interest rates are too high, leading to low growth and current account surplus. This divergence in economies led to a two-speed Eurozone.

HOW TO RESTORE COMPETITIVENESS IN THE EUROZONE?

How do Greece, Spain and Portugal restore their international competitiveness when they can't devalue the currency? The answer is to reduce inflation and wage costs. For example, the government can cut public-sector wages. But reducing wages and inflation causes even lower economic growth, and a rising real value of debt. Furthermore, to restore competitiveness by this internal devaluation can take several years of low growth and high unemployment.

EUROBOND CRISIS

Uncompetitiveness and falling exports are bad enough, but there was another complication for failing Eurozone economies.

In the Eurozone, Spain, Greece and Portugal no longer had a central bank that could decide to print euros. If a country had difficulty selling bonds — tough luck! People thought that the euro would never experience liquidity problems. The assumption was that the euro would give investors greater confidence — but that was not the case.

Investors saw rising budget deficits, but, most importantly, there was no guarantee of liquidity. As a result, investors started to sell Greek bonds, and then Irish and Spanish bonds. This caused bond yields to rise rapidly.

The fear of default in Ireland and Spain caused investors to sell bonds and demand higher bond yields. As investors sold, it caused a further loss in confidence and further selling.

When a government can't sell bonds to the private sector, it has to start cutting its budget deficit. This means austerity policies — cutting government spending and increasing taxes (see Austerity, page 226). But cutting government spending further reduces demand in the economy, leading to even lower economic growth (and lower tax revenues). Countries in the south of the Eurozone now had a combination of policies that were causing lower growth:

- Overvalued exchange rate, reducing demand for exports.
- Need to cut wages, reducing consumer confidence and spending.
- Fiscal austerity — government spending cuts and tax rises to reduce budget deficit.
- European Central Bank unwilling to pursue more unorthodox monetary policy.

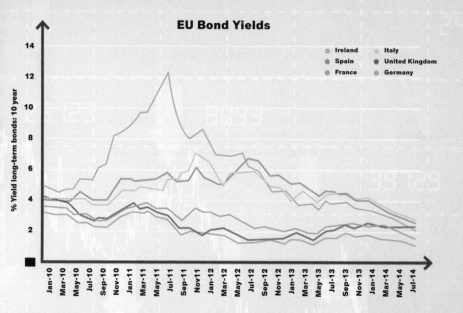

EU Bond Yields

Together, these policies caused a recession, worsening the debt crisis. Higher unemployment and lower growth led to a fall in tax revenues and a need to spend more on welfare, causing higher borrowing and therefore upward pressure on bond yields. It was a negative vicious cycle.

THE EUROPEAN CENTRAL BANK CHANGES TACK

In 2012 the European Central Bank changed policy. It stated that it was willing to provide liquidity to countries

▲ This graph shows bond yields on government debt for selected European countries. Ireland, Spain and Italy saw a sharp rise in bond yields during 2010–12, whereas German and UK bond yields remained low.

having difficulty selling bonds. In essence, it promised to act as the lender of last resort. This intervention led to falling bond yields as markets gained more confidence in Eurozone bond markets — when markets know there is a lender of last resort, bond yields stay much lower.

OPTIMAL CURRENCY ZONE

The United States has a form of a common currency — the dollar — that was introduced at the end of the 18th century. In theory, each state could have its own currency, but this would obviously create unnecessary transaction costs and harm economic activity between different states.

Because a common currency maximizes economic efficiency, it is reasonable to say the United States is an optimal currency area. Similarly, the Eurozone has a common currency used by 19 European countries. Why does a common currency work well in the United States but not so well in the Eurozone?

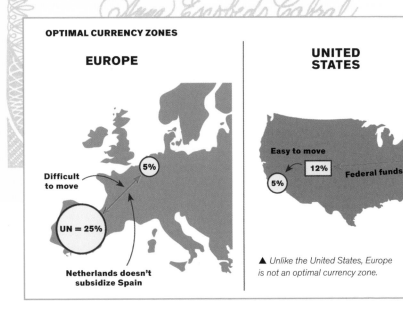

OPTIMAL CURRENCY ZONES

EUROPE

5%

Difficult to move

UN = 25%

Netherlands doesn't subsidize Spain

UNITED STATES

Easy to move

12%

Federal funds

5%

▲ *Unlike the United States, Europe is not an optimal currency zone.*

▲ *When regions in the United States suffer local recession, locals can try to move to different states or receive federal funds.*

Geographical mobility. If the state of Florida experiences a recession and high unemployment, it is relatively easy for Floridian workers to move to New York or the West Coast to find jobs. There are much greater geographical immobilities in Europe. It is not easy for an unemployed Spanish worker to move to Germany — they may not speak the language, which will lead to difficulties finding work and living accommodation.

Fiscal union. Eurozone countries don't have fiscal union. Each Eurozone country has its own budget and budget deficit. This caused tremendous pressure for southern European countries to pursue austerity in order to reduce their deficits. In the United States there is a local state budget, and there is also a federal budget that can more easily transfer spending to depressed areas of the United States. A relatively poor state like New Mexico receives a net fiscal flow (by way of federal spending raised by federal taxes) of over 250 percent of its GDP. There are some EU-wide transfers but these are a smaller share of overall GDP.

Many economists argue that for the euro to work effectively there needs to be greater fiscal union — a common budget and common bonds. But this would require considerable political will, and German voters may not be happy at the prospect of subsidizing a depressed Greek economy. In the United States, there would be greater political acceptance of wealthy New York supporting the rust belt areas of the Midwest.

ECONOMIC DEVELOPMENT

Economic development is a branch of economics concerned with how to effectively promote standards of living, social well-being and the quality as well as the quantity of economic growth.

Economic development measures a range of statistics that affect the quality of life — real GDP, mortality rates, education standards, political freedom, health care, the environment. It is possible to have a rise in GDP even though economic development does not improve. For example, if a country spends a lot of money on fighting a war, GDP may rise,

but the quality of life may significantly deteriorate. Economic development seeks to evaluate not just average incomes, but whether this growth also leads to measurable improvements in living standards.

GLOBAL INEQUALITY IS A MAJOR ISSUE

In 2015, real GDP per capita in the United States was $56,084. In Somalia, it was $474. Liberia, Congo, the Central African Republic and Somalia all had real GDP per capita of less than $1,000. This illustrates the huge inequality in global incomes. But GDP statistics don't tell the full story. Incomes are lower in developing countries, but so is the cost of living— $1 goes further in Liberia than it world in the United States. Nevertheless, even after accounting for

the differing purchasing power parity of currencies (see Glossary), there is huge inequality.

WHAT CAUSES THIS POVERTY?

In particular, investment in education, health care and transport are essential for economic development. But with very low GDP, it is hard to finance this investment.

To break the cycle of global poverty, we need policies to help increase savings, investment and the life opportunities (see Breaking the Cycle of Poverty, page 300).

NET OFFICIAL DEVELOPMENT ASSISTANCE

Government aid is classified as official aid, given with the aim of promoting economic development, at favorable loan rates. Some of the largest donors of foreign aid include:

1. United States: $31.08 billion/0.17% of GDP
2. United Kingdom: $18.70 billion/0.71% of GDP
3. Germany: $17.78 billion/0.52% of GDP
4. Japan: $9.32 billion/0.22% of GDP
5. France: $9.23 billion/0.37% of GDP
6. Sweden: $7.09 billion/1.40% of GDP

European Union: $87.64 billion

The largest single donor is the United States with $31 billionn, but this accounts for only 0.17 percent of U.S. GDP, compared to Sweden, where foreign aid is 1.4 percent of GDP.

(Figures collected by OECD's Development Assistance Committee in 2015.)

Global Poverty

1 **Low savings**

2 **Low investment**

3 **Low growth**

▲ In this cycle of global poverty, low savings mean only a small quantity of investment. This low investment leads to low growth and continued low savings.

WASHINGTON CONSENSUS

The Washington Consensus is a term used to describe a set of free-trade, market-based policies recommended by the International Monetary Fund (IMF), the World Bank and the U.S. Treasury.

According to these financial institutions, economic development requires:

1. Macroeconomic stability: monetary policy was to be used to bring inflation under control, and governments were also required to run low budget deficits.

2. Free markets: privatization was encouraged to promote innovation and greater efficiency.

3. Deregulation: markets were to be opened up to competition — both internal and external, with a reduction in tariffs to allow greater free trade.

4. Competitive/floating exchange rates.

5. Privatization: selling state-owned assets to the private sector.

For countries that required an IMF bailout, these policies were often a condition of receiving funds. Therefore, many developing economies pursued this combination of deflationary policies and free-market liberalization.

CRITICISMS OF WASHINGTON CONSENSUS

The main criticism was that these policies were not necessarily suited to all conditions and all countries — one size doesn't fit all. To reduce inflation and budget deficits often required higher interest rates and higher taxes, policies that depressed demand and often caused an economic downturn.

Supporters say this shock therapy was often necessary and that the short-term pain was worth the long-term improvements to the economy. Critics argue that it ignored social problems such as higher unemployment and cuts to social welfare reforms. Privatization and liberalization are also contentious, because of their mixed results. In Bolivia, for example, the privatization of water led to a decline in access and higher prices for the poor.

The Washington Consensus is often linked to the broader ideology of "neoliberalism" (in simple terms, a belief in unfettered free markets), though it should be noted that the English economist John Williamson, who coined the term in 1989, also advocated shifting spending to education and public infrastructure. Initially, the Washington Consensus was a combination of free-market policies and government intervention, but over time it has become more associated with the free-market approach.

INTERNATIONAL MONETARY FUND (IMF) AND WORLD BANK

• • • • • • • • •

Formed in 1944, the IMF is an international organization of 189 countries based in Washington, United States. It is primarily concerned with stabilizing the international economy. It can offer temporary funds to countries during financial and balance of payments crisis.

The World Bank, formed in 1994, is an international organization committed to reducing global poverty by offering loans and facilitating global trade and investment.

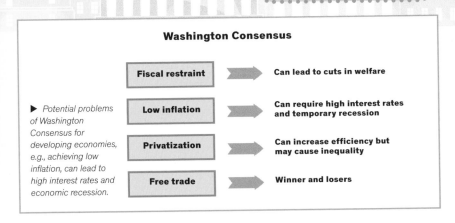

Washington Consensus

▶ *Potential problems of Washington Consensus for developing economies, e.g., achieving low inflation, can lead to high interest rates and economic recession.*

Fiscal restraint	**Can lead to cuts in welfare**
Low inflation	**Can require high interest rates and temporary recession**
Privatization	**Can increase efficiency but may cause inequality**
Free trade	**Winner and losers**

PARADOX OF PLENTY

Why are many countries that are rich in natural resources (for example, oil and diamonds) poor in terms of GDP and economic development? This is the paradox of plenty.

If an economy has plentiful natural resources we would, at first glance, expect it to prosper. The natural resources increase exports and GDP, improve tax revenue, create employment and benefit just about every macroeconomic variable there is. Yet countries that possess such resource wealth can experience many challenges.

Natural resources are often owned by companies with monopoly power, so ordinary citizens may see only a small benefit trickling down from the top. Large amounts of natural resources can be a source of civil conflict as competing factions fight for ownership. Profits from sale of diamonds and other resources can be used to finance an ongoing war, a factor in some African civil conflicts, such as that in Angola. The extraction and refinement of natural resources often require investment from foreign multinationals. These companies invest in the developing economy, but a large share of the profit is taken out of the country.

EASY WEALTH CAN ALSO CAUSE PROBLEMS

Suppose an economy discovers a plentiful supply of oil. Because the oil industry is an easy way to raise tax revenue and export revenue, the rest of the economy gets left

behind. There is little incentive to diversify the economy and develop other industries if you can produce oil. Furthermore, the discovery of oil usually leads to an appreciation in the exchange rate that can harm the competitiveness of other export industries.

In 2014–16 the rapid drop in the price of oil caused very serious problems for oil-dependent countries such as Russia and Venezuela and even rich countries like Saudi Arabia. The planning of their economies was based on the expectation of a certain amount of tax and export revenue from oil. When the oil price drops, an oil-dependent economy is ill-equipped to deal with reduced revenues.

NORWEGIAN MODEL

· · · · · · · · · ·

There is no certainly that the discovery of natural resources will cause problems or fail to alleviate poverty. Some countries, such as Norway, make great efforts to invest the proceeds of tax revenues to help improve infrastructure and save for the future. If used wisely and if everyone benefits, natural resources can help economic development and growth. Of course, without natural resources many underdeveloped economies would be even poorer.

Paradox of Plenty

Natural resources

Production dominated by foreign multinational corporation

High wealth ⟶ corruption and civil war

Economy based on mining, neglects manufacturing

Economy struggles if price of oil/diamonds collapses

▲ *Why discovering a large supply of raw materials can paradoxically create problems for economies. In other words, "easy" wealth is a mixed blessing.*

BREAKING THE CYCLE OF POVERTY

Development economics is concerned with breaking the cycle of poverty and improving living standards in developed economies.

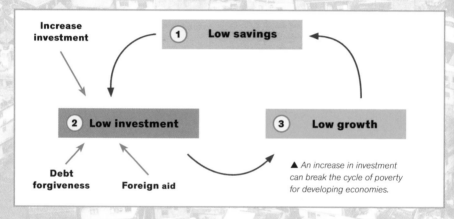

Increase investment

① **Low savings**

② **Low investment**

③ **Low growth**

Debt forgiveness

Foreign aid

▲ An increase in investment can break the cycle of poverty for developing economies.

The Washington Consensus (see page 296) is one model of development economics. Other policies include canceling debt, providing foreign aid, and capital investment.

Canceling Third World Debt. Indebted developing economies are often caught in a vicious cycle of spending a higher and higher percentage of foreign earnings on servicing debt, and therefore have less to invest in, for example, infrastructure. So-called debt

forgiveness can free up money to spend on development and social programs.

In 1996, the heavily indebted poor countries (HIPC) sought to cancel debt for 38 countries, mostly in Africa. The IMF estimated the debt relief would cost $71 billion (2007), but would help to eliminate unsustainable debt.

Foreign aid. This provides an injection of capital and funds to improve infrastructure

CHINA

• • • • • • • •

China has invested heavily in Africa in recent years, building roads and railways. It hasn't done so for altruistic reasons, but in accordance with the old economic maxim of acting in your own self-interest. China wants more efficient access to African raw materials — but the improved roads and railways and capital investment will help African development even if China leaves.

and deal with issues such as poor health care, water supply and education. Some people suggest that foreign aid can lead to donor dependency, or that it can be misplaced if aid is tied to contracts for the donor country. However, properly targeted aid can improve the fundamentals of an economy, such as infrastructure and education. **Increasing capital investment from abroad.** This can help to increase both productive capacity and incomes, creating a positive multiplier effect of rising wages and demand and incentives for companies to invest. However, it depends on the nature of capital investment. For example, multinational companies have invested in commodity extraction, but much of this investment may not trickle down to the average citizen. The owners of the resources will gain most, and profits will return to the multinational corporation in its developed economy. One of the challenges for commodity-rich developing economies is how to translate this commodity wealth into wider investment in education and infrastructure.

GLOSSARY

B

....

Balanced budget Total government spending equals taxation revenue. There is no government borrowing or surplus.

Balance of payments A country's financial transactions with the rest of the world.

Bank runs People lose faith in security of banks and demand to withdraw their savings. The spectacle of lines of people prompts others to withdraw their savings.

Bear market A market where asset prices keep falling, which encourages selling. "Bearishness" is pessimism about the market (*see* **Bull market**).

Budget surplus Government tax revenue is greater than government spending.

Bull market A market where asset prices are rising. "Bullishness" is optimism about the market (*see* **Bear market**).

Business confidence An economic indicator that measures net optimism or pessimism of business managers about the state of their business and economy.

C

....

Capital flight When assets are rapidly removed from a country, e.g., over fears of debt default or rapid devaluation (*see* **Devaluation**).

Central bank A country's national bank responsible for managing monetary policy and money supply, e.g., Federal Reserve, Bank of Canada, European Central Bank, Bank of England.

Cost–push inflation Inflation caused by an increase in the costs of production, e.g., rising oil prices, rising wages.

Current transfers An item on balance of payments (see **Balance of payments**), that involves transfers of non-capital assets, e.g., government aid or workers sending money back to country of origin.

D

Deadweight welfare loss
Loss of economic efficiency and welfare, arising from markets not reaching the socially efficient output.

Demand-side factors
Issues that impact on demand, e.g., demand for labor depends on productivity of workers.

Demand-side shock Event that causes total demand in the economy to fall, e.g., loss of confidence causes people to reduce spending.

Depreciation The value of a currency falls due to market forces.

Devaluation Government reduces the value of a currency within a fixed exchange rate system.

Developing economies
Economies with typically low income per capita, a small industrial base and limited services such as health care and education.

Division of labor
When the production process is split up so workers can concentrate on specific tasks.

Double-dip recession
A recession (fall in **GDP**) followed by recovery (rise in GDP), but then a second recession (fall in GDP.)

E

Electronically created money Central Bank increases the amount in its reserve account to effectively create money by decree.

Emerging economies
Typically, economies with middle income per capita,

a growing industrial sector and rising living standards.
Equity Fair, impartial and equal treatment.

Eurozone area Refers to the 19 EU countries (as of 2017) that use the Euro as their currency.

European Exchange Rate Mechanism (ERM) A semi-fixed exchange rate system where European countries had their currency pegged to a certain value against the D-Mark (German deutsche mark). It was the forerunner of the Euro.

F

Fiat money Currency established as legal tender by government law; usually paper money not backed by a physical commodity.

Full capacity When an economy is producing at maximum potential, i.e., no unemployment.

G

....

GDP (gross domestic product) The measure of the value of the output of goods and services produced by a country; a key indicator of a country's economic health (*see* **Nominal GDP**; **Real GDP**).

Gold standard A currency system where money can be converted for a fixed quantity of gold, and the government guarantees that fixed exchange rate.

H

....

Hot money flows Movement of capital from one country to another in response to changes in interest rates.

Hysteresis effect When a single event has a long-term impact, e.g., delayed effects of unemployment cause higher long-term unemployment.

I

....

Import tariffs Tax placed on goods imported into a country, which makes imports more expensive.

Inflation The rate at which prices in the economy increase.

Irrational exuberance A situation where investors become overly optimistic — pushing up asset prices beyond their long-term value.

L

....

Labor productivity Output per worker over a certain period of time.

Liquidity trap When injections of money into an economy fail to reduce interest rates and so make monetary policy ineffective.

M

....

Marginal cost The cost of purchasing one extra unit of a good.

Marginal income tax The income tax rate that is paid on income above a certain amount.

Marginal utility The satisfaction or happiness you gain from consuming one extra unit of a product.

Market equilibrium When supply equals demand.

Market interest rates Interest rates set by the market.

Market share The percentage of total market sales held by one firm.

Markets clear Avoiding shortages and surpluses, but attaining equilibrium where supply is equal to demand.

Means of production All the processes for making goods, including factories and shipyards.

Monetary base This is the highly liquid part of the money supply. It includes cash and banks operational deposits at the central bank. It excludes money held in saving accounts. (*see also* **Central bank**)

Money markets Financial markets where investors can gain access to highly liquid assets, enabling short-run borrowing and lending.

Money supply The total amount of money in circulation or in existence in a country.

Monopsony A situation where there is only one buyer — e.g., when an employer has market power in employing workers — enabling them to pay lower wages.

Moral hazard A situation where one person takes financial risk because someone else bears the responsibility and cost.

N

National output A measure of the total goods and services produced in an economy.

Negative equity A situation where house prices fall so homeowners have a bigger outstanding mortgage debt than what the house is worth.

Negative multiplier effect When a drop in spending or investment causes a proportionately bigger fall in economic growth due to ripple effects (*see* **Ripple effect**).

New Deal A series of interventionist economic policies (1933–38) initiated by President Franklin D. Roosevelt to alleviate the effects of the Great Depression. These included social security relief for the unemployed, public work schemes and financial reform to prevent future depressions.

Nominal GDP The monetary value of all goods and services produced in an economy, measured in current market prices not accounting for inflation (*see* **Nominal GDP**; **Real GDP**).

Nominal interest rate Current market interest rate.

Nominal wage cuts This is a decrease in the actual monetary wage paid to employees.

Nominal wages Actual monetary value of wages in current market terms.

O

Old-age dependency ratio
The percentage of elderly people as a share of the working-age population.

P

Pollution Byproduct of production, e.g., CO_2 causing global warming and damage to the environment.

Potential efficiency savings
Areas where a firm could cut costs and improve efficiency.

Primary budget surplus
A situation where, excluding debt interest payments, the government runs a budget surplus.

Primary products Raw materials that can be taken from the environment without any manufacturing process, e.g., crops, water.

Q

Quantitative easing
Central bank electronically creating money and purchasing assets to increase economic activity.

R

Real exchange rates The effective purchasing power of an exchange rate — how many goods in one country can be exchanged for goods in another.

Real GDP The value of all goods and services produced in an economy, measured in constant prices (adjusting for the effects of inflation) (*see* **GDP**; **Nominal GDP**).

Real interest rate Current market interest rate minus inflation rate.

Real value of assets
Value of assets adjusted for inflation. If house prices rise five percent, but inflation is three percent, the real rise in house prices is five minus three, equaling two percent.

Real wages Nominal wages minus inflation. Real wages show the effective purchasing power of wages.

Real wage unemployment
Unemployment caused by wages being above the market equilibrium; higher wages lead to less demand for workers.

Retained profit Profit made by a firm after paying all taxes and costs.

Ripple effect The secondary or collateral outcome of a monetary policy or economy activity.

S

Specialization When workers become skilled at particular aspects of work. In trade, specialization occurs when countries focus on certain industries or products.

Stagflation A period of high inflation, low (stagnant) economic growth and high unemployment.

Supply-side economics An economic theory that stresses the role of increasing efficiency of economy through reforms such as tax cuts and greater labor market flexibility. Downplays the role of demand-side policies.

Supply-side factors Issues that affect supply, e.g., supply of labor depends on qualifications.

T

Trading income Revenue a firm gains from business activities.

Transaction costs Costs involved in making an economic transaction or participating in a market.

V

Value-added A feature or process that helps a manufacturer to improve the quality of a product, enabling them to sell at a higher price.

W

Wage takers Where workers have little option but to accept the going wage of employers. For example, workers in a monopsony with no alternative choices of employment (see **Monopsony**).

Z

Zero-hour labor contracts Workers employed with no guarantee of the amount of paid work. Employer can give worker 40 hours, 10 hours or even zero paid hours per week.

INDEX

C

calories, 43

Canada, 228–9, 243

cancellation, barriers to, 43

capital investment, 301

Capitalism, Socialism and Democracy
(Schumpeter), 120

capitalists

Adam Smith, 15

John Maynard Keynes, 55

career breaks, 89

Carville, James, 246

cash savings, 284

CDOs (collateralized debt obligations),
266, 285

census, US, 90

central banks, 230–1

inflation, 21

China, 180–1, 236, 276, 284, 301

US national debt, 175, 190–2

Chrysler, 122–3

classical economics, 12–13

coal mining communities, 121

cobweb theory, 69

coins, 9, *see also* money

collective insanity, 148

collusion, 114–17

commodities, and environment, 184–5

Common Agriculture Policy, 70–71

Common Fisheries Policy, 63

common resources, 62

company objectives, 118–19

company profitability, 285

confidence, 212–13

conspicuous consumption, 40

containers, shipping, 103

corn syrup, 71

corporation tax, 282–3

cost-push inflation, 159, 170

creative destruction, 120–1

credit crunch (2008), 22, 138–9, 184,
266–9, 288, *see also* recession (2009)

credit rating agencies, 250

crowding out, 224–5

current account, 190

current account deficit, 100, 194–5, 202

cyclical deficit, 172

D

3D jobs, 84

debt, 228

deflation, 164–7

demand-pull inflation, 158, 159

devaluation, 202–5, 282

development economics, 23, 300–1

diamonds, 36–37

digital money, 244–5

diminishing marginal utility of wealth,
237

diminishing returns, 150–1

I

J

K

L

N

O

P

T

U

V

Veblen goods, 40–41
Veblen, Thorstein, 40
Venezuela, 299
Versailles Treaty, 162
Volker, Paul, 21
voodoo economics, 144

W

wage determination, 74–77
wage stagnation, 285
Wall Street Crash (1929), 182, 256-7
Washington Consensus, 296-7
water, 36–37, 45
The Wealth of Nations (Smith), 14–15, 276
welfare, 23
Williamson, John, 297
wisdom of the crowds, 148
work/life balance, 96, 131
workaholic rich, 97, 237
working week, 37, 86–87, 178
The 4 Hour Workweek (Ferriss), 97
World Bank, 297

X

Xenophon, 8, 78

Z

zero-hour labor contracts, 101
zero-sum game, 11

PICTURE CREDITS

All imagery copyright of Shutterstock, unless otherwise stated.

Every effort has been made to trace copyright holders and to obtain their permission for the use of copyright material. The publisher apologizes for any errors or omissions and would be grateful if notified of any corrections that should be incorporated in future reprints or editions of this book.

INTRODUCTION

pp.8, 10, 11, 12, 14, 16, 18, 20, 22, 25 Illustrations by 525 Limited – five-twentyfive.com
p.21 © Keystone-France/Gamma-Keystone/Getty Images

CHAPTER 1

pp.28, 29, 30, 33, 35, 36, 41, 45, 47, 49, 51 Illustrations by 525 Limited – five-twentyfive.com
pp.34–5 photo © Brooke Larke/Unsplash.com
p.40 © Bettmann/Getty images

CHAPTER 2

pp.45, 55, 57, 58, 61, 62, 64, 67, 68, 69, 70 Illustrations by 525 Limited – five-twentyfive.com

CHAPTER 3

pp.75, 78, 81, 83, 84, 87, 94 Illustrations by 525 Limited – five-twentyfive.com
p.77 © NurPhoto/Getty Images

CHAPTER 4

pp.100, 101, 102, 103, 105, 106, 108, 110, 114, 117, 119, 121, 122, 123 Illustrations by 525 Limited – five-twentyfive.com
p.120 © Bettmann/Getty Images

CHAPTER 5

pp.126, 129, 131, 132, 134, 135, 136, 138, 140, 142, 148, 151, 152 Illustrations by 525 Limited – five-twentyfive.com
p.127 © Hulton Deutsch/Corbis Historical/Getty Images